BOOKS AUTHORED OR CO-AUTHORED
BY ELAINE CANNON

Adversity

As a Woman Thinketh

Baptized and Confirmed: Your Lifeline to Heaven

Be a Bell Ringer

Bedtime Stories for Grownups

Boy of the Land, Man of the Lord

Corner on Youth

Eight is Great

The Girl's Book

God Bless the Sick and Afflicted

Heart to Heart

Life—One to a Customer

Merry, Merry Christmases

The Mighty Change

Mothers and "Other Mothers"

Putting Life in Your Life Story

The Seasoning

The Summer of My Content

The Time of Your Life

Turning Twelve or More: Living by the Articles of Faith

Elaine Cannon

Love You

BOOKCRAFT
Salt Lake City, Utah

Library of Congress Catalog Card Number: 90–85478

ISBN 0–88494–782–3

Second Printing, 1992

Printed in the United States of America

To the loves of my life . . .
and to
Mary Hanks Clifford and Aldon Scott Anderson
as special examples.

Love towards God and all
—Mosiah 2:4

Contents

Contents

Contents

Contents

Introduction

Is there love after divorce?

Is there love after children?

Is there true love among youth?

Is there love in the time of income tax?

Is there love among the cleanup crew after the wedding reception, the church dinner, the family reunion?

Is there love between spouses during the trauma of check reconciliation and charge-card accounting?

Is there love in the household of influenza?

Can the embers of a lively fire in the heart be stirred to flame again after a bitter misunderstanding?

Does love survive family problems, accidents, bankruptcy, disgrace, disasters such as flood, quakes, and death?

Is an exchange of tenderness possible after a court case, an estate settlement, a six-week turn with dear old Grandfather in the home, contention with teenagers, an overdraft at the bank?

Will love flourish in the midst of personal disappointment, weighty responsibility, hurt feelings, neighborhood struggles, suits over water rights and property lines (or whatever)?

Can a person really love an enemy?

The questions are relevant because God told us to love each other, to esteem those who clash with us (in other words, our enemies) as ourselves, to be like Him who loves every one. . . . Ah! Can it happen?

Yes.

God is still a God of miracles. With all things being possible through Christ, love can happen. It doesn't come with a snap of the fingers but rather through countless acts of kindness and a mind set on establishing choice relationships ranging from friendly to family to romantic to God-loving. We have but to put our heart in Christ's and reach for renewal and a healing in love.

God gave us the commandment to love one another. He gives no commandment unto the children of men unless he prepares a way for them to keep that commandment. Reading 1 Nephi 3:7 gives us greater understanding of the meaning of this truth. Meanwhile, striving to keep the commandment of loving each other is its own reward. Love fills us and life is enhanced. God's will for us is to know this joy. No matter how tough the problems, how long the day, how lonely the night, how challenging the relations, he wants us to know the joy loving brings.

All of this has been said before. Why then another book on love? Why yet another effort to explain and understand that remarkable emotion and to make it "happen" in our individual lives?

Because God told us to love.

Because love is for our own good.

Because it is very clear that in today's world many people do not really *know* love. They scarcely know *about* love. They rarely experience the full magnitude of this enriching emotion. For some, the hard things in life have made the soft things unbearable. Or a shallowness in character development renders gratitude for and joy in another human virtually impossible. Another reason is that lust and love—actually poles apart—are mistakenly considered synonymous by the foolish, who thereby are cheated out of pure love.

Real love is life. Life is eternal. The only thing keeping this most precious experience of love from flourishing in our lives is our own attitude. That is a theme that runs throughout this collection of perspectives on love—on loving and receiving and remembering love. These perspectives come from life, true stories and wise observations. There are classic essays, humorous insights, inspirational scriptures, quotable quotes, familiar lines from beloved poetry and literature. There are excerpts from learned teachers as well as comfort and guidance from the supreme example—Jesus Christ, from whom all love flows.

Love You!

The Relief Society in a certain neighborhood were gathered in their weekly meeting. Their leader spoke in tribute to them. It was a kind of off-season Mother's Day of her own making. There had been many heartbreaking situations in their area in recent weeks, and the women had responded in charitable service—they had "mothered" each other through some tough times. Charitable service had lifted the hands that hung down and strengthened the feeble knees.

In recounting these things, a mellow glow softened the lines of care in the leader's face. She described their courage, their support of each other, their selfless help given to those in need. There was money shared for school shoes for a neighbor's child; meals in and laundry out on behalf of a young mother threatened with a miscarriage of twins; a fund-raising for a family's last vacation together before the father's terminal cancer changed their lives forever; guest quarters provided for visiting relatives during wedding festivities in a financially stressed widow's family, and catering service for the reception, as well; a daily delightful deluge of cards, notes of love, and "chin-up" surprises sent to the wife of a newly excommunicated errant husband; a cleanup crew, from among themselves and their families, organized to scour through a family home before the mother of many returned from being hospitalized for weeks after a fiery car smashup; the sensitive and practical outreach extended to an older single girl who was squeezed out of her job and had no resources to fall back on.

And there was more—an incredible outpouring of hearts, investments of self, and fasting and praying for heavenly support in behalf of others. The leader became emotional as she looked into their faces, remembering. Their loving service was counted as nothing short of "inimitable blessings" for their neighborhood. Nothing was so terrible when it was shared with friends. The leader emphasized the privilege she felt was hers just to associate with them.

At last she finished lamely but eloquently, "I have no other words, no sweeter feeling to share with you except . . . I love you. *Love you!*"

President Ezra Taft Benson was in the hospital recovering from surgery during October 1990 general conference. The first session opened with President Gordon B. Hinckley speaking to Church members on behalf of President Benson. Then President Hinckley said he spoke for all members of the Church within the sound of his voice. He said, "Our dear friend and leader, our President and prophet, we love you!"[1]

And You!

"Love you!" promised the sweet young thing to her boyfriend, who was off to the wars, to school, to fill a mission—whatever. "Love you forever," and she meant it, too, only she married someone else who came home first. But she loved him, too.

"Love you!" The young husband flung the words out as he looked over the top of the car at his wife on the porch—wrapper and scraggly hair notwithstanding.

"Love you back!" she answered, blowing a kiss.
That's called setting the thermostat early for later warmth.

"Love you!" cooed the teenage daughter, twining her arms around her father's neck. "And thanks, dear Moneybags, for the backing." The father knew he had been set up and robbed. But he had gone into the deal willingly just to hear those words from that particular beautiful young woman.

"Love you!" The priesthood leader slowly shook his head in wonderment. "Brethren, if one man can say that to another, this is the time to say it. We do love you for pitching in and making the difference. We could not have coped with the fire in the church had you not responded to the network call. And in such willing haste, such tireless work, such generous sharing of equipment and funds! Thank you."

"Love you!" the young grandson said across the miles. And the grandmother felt mellow inside because the family tradition had reached one more little person in their posterity. "Love you!" instead of "good-bye" when a telephone conversation was wrapped up was like a comforting squeeze of the arm, a firm handclasp, a finger dangled across the back of one's neck, a kiss on the cheek, a tender pat on the head.
Yes, *"Love you!"* And you and you and you!

The Proverbial Sparrow

God loves us every one. In the loveless days, take comfort that God loves us. Remember again that he has told us he even loves every common sparrow and notes its fall. Why not, then, us? And if

God loves us does it matter, in the long run, what others feel at the moment?

Read again this passage found in Luke 12:6–7, "Are not five sparrows sold for two farthings, and not one of them is forgotten before God? . . . Even the very hairs of your head are all numbered. Fear not therefore: ye are of more value than many sparrows."

This charming nursery verse is food for thought, too:

> Said the robin to the sparrow,
> "I should really like to know
> Why these anxious human beings
> Rush about and worry so."
> Said the sparrow to the robin,
> "Friend, I think that it must be
> That they have no Heavenly Father
> Such as cares for you and me."

The wonderful comfort about God's love is that it often comes spilling over into our lives at moments when we feel no more important than the proverbial sparrow.

I'm thinking of the night I lay stricken in an illness that had plagued me for weeks, leaving me weak from fever and pain. Prayer and priesthood blessings notwithstanding, I had not been able to "rise and walk." This late-hour silent cry from my sickbed was more a plea than a prayer: "O God, dear God, I can't take this much longer! Bless me. Bless me, please!"

And the clear answer came into my mind, crowding all else out: "I already have."

Silence. My heart began to pound with understanding. I had already been blessed by Him! I had not died. I had survived long enough for the doctors to finally diagnose my disease. I had been sustained.

And then it came—that incredible, encompassing flood of warmth . . . light . . . peace . . . gratitude. And love.

Example of Loving

You know—experience has engraved this upon your grateful heart—that a friend is someone who stands by when everyone else has moved on. Henry David Thoreau said that we don't need to wish for friends to feed and clothe our bodies—neighbors are kind enough for that—but to do "the like office to our spirit. For this, few are rich enough, however well disposed they may be."

After all, to be that kind of friend is a blessing to the world.

The boy suddenly left the side of the casket and ran to a nearby garden for a fistful of flowers to place in the empty hands of the lady lying there. He'd loved her in life. She was his friend. They'd shared countless kindnesses and much laughter. He was five and she was seventy-five. He was an example.

And now this from the thoughtful pen of Dorothy Brown Thompson:

> Just why should friends be chronological,
> Fraternal friends, or pedagogical,
> Alike in race or taste or color—
> It only makes the meetings duller!
> Unclassified by tribe or steeple,
> Why shouldn't friends be merely people?[2]

In Heaven with You

Love at its best, God-blessed and satisfying, is about heaven. At this point it is heaven on earth, to be sure, but it is all we know of heaven, yet.

There once was a perky three-year-old, wise beyond her years and charming already, too. She's grown now into the lovely lady her beginnings promised. What makes her memorable is something that happened when she was three and living in London with her parents.

Following a big meeting of people who love the Lord, she stood beside a woman who had just given a talk. To the little girl it must have seemed like a long talk, but as the crowd pressed about the woman, a veritable stranger to the child, the little one reached to tug at the lady's skirt. It caught the woman's attention and she looked down into a face, small and radiant, full of innocence and love. The child's eyes held the woman's as she in her small voice said, "I love you. I want to be in heaven with you."

And the speaker knew that in that sentence was the sermon she wished she'd given.

People of all kinds—of various age, color, temperament, station and pursuit in life, but of purity and acceptance, too—loving other people . . . how good it can be!

Love loves anyway. The best love is expressed when people put their hands in God's and do helpful service to others in his name. They live so close to Jesus that the Holy Spirit spills over and bathes and washes and enriches and heals those they serve.

Remember the woman who touched the hem of the Savior's robe? She had been ill for many years and had spent all that time with many physicians in an effort to stop the "issue of blood," but it had become worse. She had heard of Jesus and said to herself, "If I may touch but his clothes, I shall be whole" (Mark 5:28). She pushed through the crowd from behind Jesus to secretly touch his robe.

Jesus sensed the woman's presence. While other people merely pressed about him, she *connected* in faith. And Jesus healed her, saying, "Thy faith hath made thee whole; go in peace, and be whole of thy plague" (Mark 5:34).

We who are trying to be like Jesus, who have taken upon us his name, his work, and his ways can reach out in need to others and receive their healing love and help. We can give love and help to those who touch our lives.

Of such is the kingdom of heaven.

6

Love's Surprise

You've heard some lovers insist that if you don't hear bells when you are kissed, better get your ears checked—or a new romantic interest.

Another opinion on the matter is that love comes on the sly, slips in almost unnoticed. One day you are strangers, or friends at best, and the next you are in love. Bells or not!

This surprise element of love is one of its better properties. It happens all along the way of life, on every level of loving, too. And then happy days are here again.

For example, as a child you are up in front of the schoolroom with your visual aids for a presentation. You awkwardly spill the stuff on the floor. The class laughs uproariously. Your friend steps forward to help gather the pieces. Oh, how you appreciate that friend at that moment—to not be alone in humiliation! And your heart brims over.

For example, as a teenager at the stake dance you dance with a boy who is shorter than you. He'd been a shadow on the block before he dared to seek you out from the wall of flowers who weren't dancing. You laugh together about your high-low condition. Having known each other forever has little influence on the magic of the moment when you realize flexibility and good humor can turn two sticks into the best of friends. By the last dance your hearts are pounding.

For example, as a young adult you've been part of a large group of guys and gals who "do things together." No dates. No progress. A lot of feeding the boys. Plenty of seeing the girls get home safely. But twosomes? Fat chance. Everyone is just friends. But then a new committee is formed, and in this safe harbor two of you get to know each other as good thinkers, good sports, good workers, good catches! Like that, it happens. You are happy and unself-conscious. You give of yourself without chalking up score. That's right—unsuspecting a moment before, now it happens. You are happier. Love does that to you. And so does just a good friendship.

A Particular Person

Why is it that out of all the faces in the world *that* face holds special appeal? How interesting that of all the people in all the world two paths cross, something clicks, and a friendship is born! And isn't it interesting that there are so few who become especially dear? It has nothing really to do with how that person looks, what he/she does or says, or even how frequently association happens. That particular person, come what may, matters to us in a singular way and will forever!

There is something so sound about Arthur Christopher Benson's perspective about friendship: "Who shall explain the extraordinary instinct that tells us, perhaps after a single meeting, that this or that particular person in some mysterious way matters to us? I confess that, for myself, I never enter a new company without the hope that I may discover a friend, perhaps *the* friend, sitting there with an expectant smile. That hope survives a thousand disappointments."

There are some people who have hearts large enough and perhaps the enviable expansive disposition that provide them with a wide circle of friends. They go on multiplying relationships till the grave. How rich is such a life!

Helen Keller was an impressive human being. Her writings include a paragraph on the subject of what a particular person can do to change the feel and flow of a day: "There are red-letter days in our lives when we meet people who thrill us like a fine poem, people whose handshake is brimful of unspoken sympathy and whose sweet, rich natures impart to our eager, impatient spirits a wonderful restfulness. . . . Perhaps we never saw them before and they may never cross our life's path again; but the influence of their calm, mellow natures is a libation poured upon our discontent and we feel its healing touch as the ocean feels the mountain stream freshening its brine."[3]

Let us not turn this into such a hunt for a special friend—that particular person—that we forget the blessed relationships that are ours now. So much of what another can do for us in satisfying a need in a relationship hinges on our own attitude—our sunshine-in-our-heart demeanor or our down-in-the-mouth disposition. "Until the real thing comes along," as the old song wails, we can be glad for what we have in friendship, love, or a lasting relationship.

How great if "that particular person" is counted as spouse, child, parent! But if not, how blessed to find a particular person who sails your ship, pushes your button, starts your motor, pacifies your ugly uglies!

The Habit of Love

Some may insist that saying "Love you!" every time you turn around, turn away, say hello, say good-bye, leave or come, weep or laugh—some say it's ruining a good thing. "Love you!" becomes just another buzz word. "Love you!" gets to be so common it loses its meaning. Some might suggest that using the phrase "Love you!" so easily, frequently, lightly, jauntily becomes . . . ah . . . nothing. Nothing? The most treasured feeling remembered in a quick exchange between two people under whatever appropriate circumstances? Nothing? At the very least it is a pleasant exchange between people who have some tie to each other, some social memory or warmth, pleasantness, necessity in each other's lives.

Nothing? Just a habit? Well, what a habit to have! We all should be so caught up, enslaved in niceness!

The habit of love can be learned as love is practiced and performed. When people learn how it feels to say the words without discomfort, the chances of getting other kinds of words of love expressed are increased. Love is a four-letter word, too, but on the golden side of the spelling list.

And it could be added, "Hallelujah! The world is turning into a better place." No matter who wars with whom upon which oil field or sand dune, there are yet those dedicated to keeping alive one of God's choice gifts to mankind—the right and opportunity to relate to each other in love.

Saying so may make it so.

Establishing Ties

We've talked of the near miracle of happening on or suddenly finding a particular person who is different for us from all others—someone who matters eternally, forever.

"Finding" admits chance. It may or may not happen.

But what of cultivating or taming to form a special relationship?

What about establishing such ties that neither party in the relationship can be discounted—ever? Ah, now we are talking building heaven on earth!

Such associations should be God-blessed, God-tamed, if you will.

Antoine de Saint-Exupéry's insightful story called *The Little Prince* elaborates on this idea. The little prince is planet hopping in a grand adventure. At one point he is feeling sad and lonely. Then he meets a fox, and he asks the fox to play with him.

> "I cannot play with you," the fox said. "I am not tamed."
> "Ah! Please excuse me," said the little prince.
> But, after some thought, he added:
> "What does that mean—'tame'?" . . .
> ". . . It means to establish ties."
> " 'To establish ties'?"
> "Just that," said the fox. "To me, you are still nothing more than a little boy who is just like a hundred thousand other little boys. And I have no need of you. And you, on your part, have no need of me. To you, I am nothing more than a fox like a hundred thousand other foxes. But if you tame me, then we shall need each other. To me, you will be

unique in all the world. To you, I shall be unique in all the world. . . . It will be as if the sun came to shine on my life. I shall know the sound of a step that will be different from all the others."[4]

Consider the happy state people would be in if parents established ties with children. If children worked at establishing ties with parents! And what if teachers of classes established ties of a kind with each student? Consider the advantages to human dignity and happiness, to pleasure in the workday world if a boss established ties with coworkers and the people on the job established appropriate ties with their employers.

When we make the effort to *know* each other we're taking that step. We can find out about birthdays, family members and makeup, favorite foods, books being read, standards from which they can't be budged and why such beliefs are so important to them. We can be sensitive to troubles, cycles, what stirs anger and causes irritation. What adventures have highlighted the lives of these people we are relating to and want to be friends with? What places have they lived and worked in?

Taming—establishing ties—makes sound sense, doesn't it? Even if friendship with a "particular one" doesn't develop, warmth and respect can be generated among associates at home, work, school, church, and the grocery store.

Remember, this isn't about missionary work, stopping the climbing divorce rate, or stomping out war. Yet!

This is about people reaching out to other people. People honoring the humanness of people. People understanding people. People beginning to like people. And becoming friends. Maybe loved ones.

And then, let there be peace on earth!

Thank Heaven for Friends!

Friendship becomes a valuable emotion as time moves on. Even in youth there usually is more comfort, more peace, and fewer emotional assaults between friends than lovers, so-called. If chemistry and circumstance move a couple to marriage, surely friendship must develop between them for true satisfaction and staying power to exist in their relationship. One cannot be in a state of sexual excitement all the time. And no doubt that is contrary to the usual picture painted by the media.

Some people are natural peacemakers, people pleasers, friends. Others of us learn with maturity to be more generous in extending friendship to others, because experience lets us judge others more charitably. We admire mankind on the broad scale as we watch good people on the home front battle the dishonest, the power-hungry, the aggressive tyrants, even terrorists. We melt before the courage of individuals meeting the daily shocks in life. And we find that having our own way, keeping our own opinion up front or insisting upon its acceptance with others, is selfish and shallow and futile. It is simply more pleasant to listen and learn—even if we go home and do and think as we please. Idealism is essentially a luxury few can afford socially. Emerson had the opinion that it is easy to live in the world after the world's standards and that it is also easy to live alone with our own; the challenge, he said, is to keep our standards while living in the world. The scripturalist will recognize Christ's admonition to his disciples about living in the world but being not of it.

Well and good, but in the name of friendship, of recognizing the divine in each person, of accepting their views, their beliefs, their right to appear socially with dirt under their nails and cobwebs in their brains—in the name of friendship we forgive such differences and embrace the beautiful about them.

We cry the poignant plea, "Oh, let me be patient with others as I pray for their patience with me, while we grow in perfection." But again, perfection doesn't require FAX copies among people. Thank heaven for friends and that we are spared such boredom of being all exactly alike.

What Gift for You, My Friend?

Two pushing-past-middle-age gentlemen friends had a reunion at a social gathering lately. Living in different states now, they were glad to be together informally. Arms around each other, smiles wide, eyes alight with remembrance of very choice times in the past —ball teams, missions, singing groups, and courting days.

"What can I do for you?" one asked the other. "What can I give you?"

"Sing!" someone interrupted. "Sing your duet." And they did, hesitant and feeling each other's pace at first but suddenly bursting forth in good voice and close harmony their theme song from other days, "Two Boys from Utah." And the onlookers were mellowed, softened in their own remembering of friendships while enjoying the awareness that good relationships last, no matter the distance in time and miles and the demanding public responsibilites that burden successful people.

Coworker, neighbor, sister, brother, tennis partner, child, spouse, doctor, church worker . . . *friend,* because the elements were right when circumstance brought togetherness. Association ripened relationship.

Time makes friendship valuable—time filled with countless small favors, efforts, demands, and moments of being there. Chemistry, too, of course. Friends, however, need not have all that much in common, except each other.

And with such a friend, so long enjoyed, the fact of gratitude swells into action sometimes. What to give such a friend—in thanks, in love, in a gesture to brighten a life, lighten a load, or simply underscore value in relationship. Like flowers blooming better with cultivation and care, so a friendship that is nurtured now and then seems sweeter.

What can we give a friend?

A song, yes. Some old sheet music found in a house move. A hymnal with a favorite message marked. A duplicate tool for her son's first home. A first violet of the season. The last rose of summer. A volunteer Potawatomi plum tree with its young roots balled for easy transplant and a jar of new jelly to sell the deal. Mint and rosemary for her herb garden. A cassette of mood music. News clippings proving that the goodness of people still exists. A quote suitable for her presentation at literary club or church.

Taxi service.

Pastry when her children are coming to visit.

Pastry even when they're not!

Red peppers from the garden and chili sauce from the pot.

Strong back, ready hands when there is crash cleanup needed.

Lemonade delivered on a hot day. Steamy spiced cider on a cold one.

A bouquet—even if it is cut from a garden catalogue—when she's honored for birth or accomplishment. A new scent for self-esteem, such as lavender in a lotion or gardenia in a bar soap.

A scriptural passage relevant to current need. One that is inspiring for any time. Another that points a certain way. One that reminds and comforts. Still another that underscores hope. Etcetera! Each written out and sent daily for prolonged support.

A bank, for a paper weight or for quarter saving, but proof that you bank on her, that she can bank on you.

That's it . . . any small thing that underscores a choice relationship full of trust, humor, support, and availability whenever.

Drawn In by Love

In the beginning Virginia stayed on the front porch to visit with her hesitant new neighbor. Even though she wasn't invited in, Virginia smiled, expressed an interest in the family, and shared a truth from the gospel of Jesus Christ.

Time passed and these two women became better friends. At last Virginia was not only invited in, she was urged to stay. Still during this time the woman never came to church, but she became accustomed, even a little interested, in Virginia's spiritual messages.

The years passed. Families grew, crises were shared and troubles overcome, youth turned to middle age, loaves were exchanged at Christmas and meals at the time of sickness. But the woman still did not step inside the church, nor was there any social life shared by these two poles-apart people.

But love was there. Real affection had grown out of countless small acts of kindness, first from Virginia alone but then taken up in a small way by the neighbor who was learning.

When terminal illness struck the visiting teacher it was impossible for her to make the calls. *This* neighbor came to Virginia! She came more often than a usual Relief Society visit. Her compassion and eagerness to be close to this lovely woman brought her to the house of sickness on a regular basis. In the end, when others had wearied of well-doing, this faithful friend gave richly of her time to care for Virginia—to sit with her and stroke her hand in the last stages of coma. When death came she wept the real tears of personal loss. Virginia in a persistent outreach of love had drawn in the neighbor and led her to God.

13

Walk in Love

To take another look at love through the scriptures broadens our perspective as it narrows our resolve to be more like Jesus. For it was he who walked in love, who washed the feet—who removed the sandals and washed the dusty feet—of his close associates! He gently permitted people to love him in whatever way they were capable of at a given moment—Martha, Magdalene, John, Joseph of Arimathaea.

We understand that man's expression of love should go toward God first and toward our fellow human beings. When we show forth love toward God with all our heart, might, mind, and strength and in the name of Jesus Christ serve him by loving and teaching and helping others, we will be filled with God's love. We are changed.

We become anxiously interested in helping others feel and know what we feel and know. We are conscious of all God has done for us in the smallest ways—ways that escaped our attention and thanksgiving before. We are repentant—we want to be what we need to be in order to make heaven on earth and to qualify to be with our Father in the next life.

It is our goal to follow the admonition in Ephesians 5:1–2 to be "followers of God, as dear children; and walk in love."

Service and Love

The world, as well as the neighborhood, is indeed a more comfortable place when charitable hearts of neighbors, friends, family members, lovers are expressed toward each other through helpful acts—all of which is a fulfillment of the commandment, "Thou shalt love the Lord thy God with all thy heart, with all thy might, mind, and strength; and in the name of Jesus Christ thou shalt serve him" (D&C 59:5). And it follows that when we serve others we also serve Jesus.

Over the years in movies and music there have been variations on the themes of service and love. Lovers promise to capture the moon or gather the stars. In a movie made many years ago called *Now, Voyager,* Bette Davis and Paul Henreid play a scene with an important message on love. Paul's character is a married man; Bette's character is a professional, single woman. Their appreciation for each other is deep. Paul speaks about giving her the moon, if he could. Bette replies most poignantly, "Don't let's ask for the moon when we have the stars." The message is clear—enough is as good as a feast. Gratitude, service in love. No home-wreckers these!

One passionate young woman wrote her missionary boyfriend that she would gladly crawl through a forest on her knees for him should the need arise. And at the moment she meant it; love stirred her, lifted her to heights of unselfishness and sacrifice she simply hadn't understood before.

Remember Tevye in *Fiddler on the Roof* plaintively singing to his wife, "Do you love me?" Her answer is the practical side of love, proof of feeling through a listing of services rendered — washed shirts, laundered socks, ready meals.

Is there a musical, a movie, a song, a verse where the wife asks the husband for proof of love and he responds with a list of *his* services rendered? What of devotion to nine-to-five workdays and more? What of sharing the paycheck, so hard come by, with a grasping family of consumers waiting for it at the other end? What of no time for self-indulgence in the fact of long days in the marketplace, evenings in the meeting halls, and after-hours stints as handyman and keeper of accounts? No jewels, flowers, dinners on the town, perhaps, but evidence of love.

There seems to be an application here of the scriptural account in Acts 3:1–7. At the temple gate Peter and John are confronted by the cripple asking for alms. "And Peter, fastening his eyes upon him with John, said, Look on us. And he gave heed unto them, expecting to receive something of them. Then Peter said, Silver and gold have I none; but such as I have give I thee: In the name of Jesus Christ of Nazareth rise up and walk. And he took him by the right hand, and lifted him up: and immediately his feet and ankle bones received strength."

A remarkable, moving truth about love — one may not have "silver and gold" (lucrative employment, glamorous trappings, sex appeal) but what the loving partner *does* have and *will* give in love and service can make all the difference. The healing, the filling with love, comes when such a gift is received as "all there is." And it is enough.

There is much to be said, after all, for the degree of comfort that comes in service-oriented relationships; we make life easier for each other by our small (or grand) acts of love and service. One woman confessed that, as a young bride, sleeping in had been her thing. Yet in that beginning season of marriage she rousted herself from bed to make breakfast for her spouse because she wanted to see him, to be close with him before a day of separation. A little breakfast with a lot of loving was the pattern. As the years passed, duty was the motivation. She made breakfast for him in order to prove her worth as a homemaker. Later, she served him especially structured, balanced breakfasts—for health's sake. Keep him alive! He's an asset!

They're alone together again, these days, and she prepares the first meal of the day in tenderness, because she has come to cherish him so much she simply cannot do enough for him.

How *love*-ly!

One learns to love God in much the same way—for whatever reasons, at whatever stage, always moving in the direction of awareness of the goodness of God and the beauty of life enjoyed because of such association and its accompanying outpouring, whatever that might be.

Love Somebody!

Love for the joy of loving.
Don't just stand there—love somebody!
Love God's creations.
Love the gift of life.

Send out the signals to mankind that you are willing to make hearts happy. And if you want to love some particular person, face the moment and do it! Such affectionate outpouring may not be returned either by people or creations, but you'll feel better for the effort.

Making oneself one with God's nature conjures up the elements within us in such a way that we lay ourselves open to love from others. Thinking love, feeling love, sharing love, being grateful to God for love's warm healing and comforting spell actually bring a change in one's physical appearance, behavior, and general health. So say many studies. This is also the testimony of thoughtful people who understand about loving God, his creations, and all mankind, and about having self-respect.

Fyodor Dostoevsky had opinions and wisdom to share on the great emotions and moments of life. Here is one such gem: "You must love all that God has created, both his entire world and each single tiny sand grain of it. Love each tiny leaf, each beam of sunshine. You must love the animals, love every plant. If you love all things you will also attain the divine mystery that is in all things. For then your ability to perceive the truth will grow every day, and your mind will open itself to an all-embracing love."

On the other hand, if you don't love, life can be sunless, flowers appear pale, and animals simply seem nuisances. The consciousness of loving and being loved brings a warmth and richness to life like nothing else.

As children, many of us learned these stunning lines: "I lived for myself, I thought for myself, for myself, and none beside—just as if Jesus had never lived, as if He had never died."

Some people, for whatever reason, put off loving, are uncomfortable with closeness and affectionate relationships. But the postponement of loving until "someday" is the opposite of living!

Love is God's gift. If you need help, pray to him for heart softening, or a change in perspective, patience until the object of your affection is perfect. Perfect? Perfection is for heaven, isn't it?

But with God nothing is impossible. Where God is, love is also. Clichés, it may seem, but with God's power love comes. Perhaps it will follow a series of challenges that shape your soul; then the flood of emotion can come.

16

Minnie Cakes

Mother was the only lady we knew who had a cake decorating set—a small aluminum cannister with a handle that worked up and down inside it much like an old-fashioned butter churn. There were three interchangeable tips through which the frosting was squeezed. There was a tip for leaves. One to make roses, and one for making loopy lines and writing names, greetings, dates, or whatever on the top of the cake. It was a fabulous invention in those days.

Mother's name was Minnie and so we called the cakes that she made and decorated for our family birthdays "Minnie cakes." Little did we know back then what buzzwords *mini* and *maxi* would become down through the years.

Then one day mother got the idea of making a cake for "Uncle Willie," the man who had been our milkman for many, many years. The new one told us one day that Uncle Willie was living alone in a one-room apartment on Canyon Road near City Creek. Mom decided he needed a cake. He had done so much for us over the years beyond the call of milk delivery.

For one thing, he spread joy. He made us all feel special, liked, valuable, important, loved—whatever you want to call it. We felt really good when Uncle Willie drove up, parked by our house, and said, "Well, good morning you lively scallywags!" And he laughed a hearty laugh as he slapped the nearest one on the shoulder. We liked him, all right, and when, just for us, he chipped off suck-size chunks from the big blocks of ice, we thought he was the next best thing to Santa Claus. Sometimes he would give us a bottle of left-over thick cream with the instruction to take it right in to Mother and have her freeze it up with the raspberries from the garden or the apricots, soaked in a little sugar, from the tree.

Sometimes he helped Mother with the clothesline that sagged under the weight of Monday's wash. Sometimes he helped us kids get the cat down from the telephone pole.

Now he'd become ill, a widower living a lonely, loveless life in his little room down the hill by the canyon stream.

The cake was made and frosted, decorated and boxed in a high hatbox, standard equipment in every household closet back then. I was elected to deliver it to his door.

I was eleven years old. His apartment was by my grade school, so I knew the way.

It was not fun. I couldn't find a friend to go with me. I was hampered by the precious hatbox. Therefore I couldn't make the long walk from Capitol Hill to Canyon Road more interesting as we did going home from Lafayette School on North Temple and State Street. We'd climb up the long flights of stairs to the hill houses along State Street. Then we'd swoosh back down on the narrow cement "slides" banking the steps. Tough on shoes and bloomer bottoms, but great sport—except when one is carrying a cake in a hatbox.

At last I arrived at Uncle Willie's room. And something wonderful happened. The sick old man acted glad to see me. He even remembered who I was. Then when I gave him the box— pushed it on him, because he seemed shy about taking it—he was all speechless and giggly. Then when he opened the box and saw that decorated cake he exploded, "Mercy!" His cheeks crinkled into a kind of smile. His mattery eyes misted.

His voice was really scratchy as he read the writing on the cake: "Happy Birthday Uncle Willie. We love you!"

I never felt so good! My heart was pounding. I had a new sensation, too. I really loved Uncle Willie. I wanted to hug him, because I had brought happiness to his door.

A Minnie cake was subsequently made for the new Jewish convert from England who had startled our conservative, all-white, all-Christian neighborhood by moving in among us.

One was made for the handicapped child who was my age but

was injured at birth so that she seemed like a forever infant. One was made—just as a surprise to brighten a grey day—for the lady whose husband left her for another woman (so we heard the older folks say). One was made every year for the mongoloid boy.

And I got to deliver the cakes. I received the joy. I learned the lesson about loving people you aren't related to and how little it takes to make others feel wanted, needed, and loved.

No, it didn't take much doing at all to bring such joy. After all, Mother made the Minnie cakes.

17

Love among Ashes

He was like a petite candle now—a white birthday candle —waxen, narrow, unyielding. Death hovered. Surely the struggle soon would be over for them both. He was past caring about being an imposition to others, so mighty was the battle to endure pain and the humiliation of bodily malfunction. She, worn with care-giving in place of her mother who had long since succumbed to an accident was emotionally depleted as well. She had set her own life aside to be nursemaid to a father who had become a pitiful stranger to her.

She swabbed his mouth, lips, gums, teeth against the ravages of drugs. She used the electric razor lightly, skilled now in man's rightful art. As she brushed his sparse hair she remembered threading her little-girl fingers through luxuriant dark waves. Now there were only memories and wisps and shags of lifeless hair white as the scalp. She recalled the childish delight in smoothing his thick moustache before he laughingly snapped at her fingers. Now thin gruel smeared his upper lip, spills from her spoon-feeding.

She took the damp washcloth and gently wiped his face. Who was this? Where was the man who had been her dear father, so beloved, in fact, that no other man could measure up, qualify as life's companion? She searched for familiarity and comfort among unruly eyebrows too heavy for a forehead taut in death and cheekbones, jaw, and nose unduly protruding—a stranger's face, though she'd cared for it weeks into months.

As the cloth pressed past the sunken eyes they opened and caught hers. There in that instant—communication! It was her father inside that wasted body. The soul of the stranger she had been caring for was indeed familiar to her, and in a wonderful exchange of love their eyes brimmed, the pulse in each quickened, the press of cheek against cheek was real and rewarding. In seconds she knew an incredible gratitude and an outpouring of pure love. Then he was gone.

Life is made of such moments of love which turn proverbial ashes to a harness of hope that one day we'll enjoy that same sociality again, beyond whatever veil separates here and There!

O Day of Days

Was it spring or winter when first we met?

Was it a darkened parking plaza, the chapel lobby, or a fragrant hill?

And were we young and innocent, or old, knowing, mature, and ripe to sense the goodness in each other? Does it matter? Love is ageless.

Strange that every detail of that meeting should be so vivid, engraved upon the heart, but in trying to describe the scene each detail suddenly becomes a blur in the face of the spiritual impact as hands were clasped.

But for all that, and for all that never could be, it was a day of days in a stack of calendars.

It is a marvelous need of our eternal nature to love something, and we are molded by what we love and what we do about that love. How kind are we? How pure? How filled with gratitude for shared association—or for simply crossing beautiful paths, with one of God's best, for a time? After all, because we walk hard and humble paths, shall we not pick a plum or two?

Young Love

We hear young love spoken of as if it were a fact of years, meant only for those under twenty. But let us speak of it as a feeling of the heart. How sweet it is at any age, because of its freshness, mystery, excitement! However, the driving force behind such excitement can spell trouble! By request, included here are some excerpts on the subject from the author's book *Be a Bell Ringer* (Bookcraft, 1989):

Let's get one thing out of the way—when it comes to boys and girls, male and female, men and women, guys and gals, or any other combination, sex is a sin unless you are legally and lawfully married.

Let's clear up a point about sin.

Sin is forbidden by God because it is hurtful. It is not hurtful because it is forbidden. The best counsel you can get is not to sin.

The Lord has told us "to suffer" (that is, to allow) no unclean ideas even to enter our hearts or heads. They mean trouble. He says, "For it is better that ye should deny yourselves of these things, wherein ye will take up your cross, than that ye should be cast into hell" (3 Nephi 12:30).

In other words, don't even *think* about sinning! You don't even tease or fool around with the sacred issues of God. That is, if you are the kind of quality person you seem to be.

Some may question how anything so fun, so natural, so accepted, can be a sin? Don't forget, it is a sin only under the wrong conditions. This is so to

—protect the innocent;

—keep procreation on a lofty level; and

—preserve God's purposes in his perfect plan for us.

You see, the first two great sins are murder and adultery (or sex out of wedlock, remember). Think about it this way: both of these actions mock God. Murder is taking life. And that is God's business. Sex is the way life is invited or how babies are created. If this is done under conditions God has not authorized it is a mockery to him. It is taking God's role into your own hands to fool around with life and death—or anything like unto it.

What about birth control? Listen, would you tease somebody by drifting a sharp knife across his throat or playing gun games? No! Though this is not murder, it is pretending . . . and it is frightening. The image carries into sexual activities. Pretending or "anything like unto it," as the scriptures say, is understandably displeasing to God.

Sex is for a wife and her husband. It is the way a couple can develop oneness. It is saved for marriage for the sake of the couple and the children that may come to that couple. It is the ultimate act of intimacy that God has provided to unite a certain special woman with her certain special man so that they come to know each other as they are not known to anybody else. Also, so that they may have the incredible blessing of being earthly parents to others of Heavenly Father's spirit children.

Such a sacred thing as a new spirit's coming from heaven to earth should be surrounded by purity, responsibility, tenderness, maturity, and God's blessings and love. Don't you agree?

Consider yourself warned and forewarned.

The rules of the Plan of Life require *obedience* or *punishment* for your own good. And there is good reason.

You see, no unclean thing can dwell in our loving, caring Heavenly Father's presence. He wants us back home. He wants us to make it, and someday we all want to do that. Heaven is where joy and fulfillment will come to us. Heaven is perfection. Sin stifles perfection and brings guaranteed pain.

As for today, here on earth, no unclean person—such as one who has had sex out of wedlock, for example—can keep the companionship of the Holy Ghost. Once you lose that precious gift given you at the time of baptism and confirmation, you are in trouble. You no longer have that special, sacred, sure guide to what is right and wrong. Then you are in *real trouble*. You'll make all kinds of mistakes that will pile trouble on your back and bring misery to your entire family before you can cry real tears.

20

Love in the Time of Saltair

Summer and Saltair were synonymous. Romance was the name of the game.

All winter long that great resort on the briny shore of Great Salt Lake stood stark, dark, boarded against the damaging salt storms, and ignored.

But come summer that enormous Moor-like castle, housing the largest open-air dance floor west of the Mississippi, ruled the western horizon of Salt Lake City, Utah. Romantic couples flocked there, as did the migrating fowl, who used the wide balustrade as a way station. The twinkling lights outlining Saltair's exotic onion turrets and towers were a beacon on the shoreline and a lure to dance lovers of all ages.

The elements conspired to give Saltair resort its remarkable and romantic setting from the turn of the twentieth century until it burned down in the seventies. Magnificent sunsets, with colors prismed through salt-reflected fantasy shades, fell onto the pavilion itself. The unique lingering twilight stirred simple, good feelings or the serious business of love. But the favorite time was before the last dance, when there was a moon to watch as it hung orange over the smelter to the south. And just north of Saltair, in the sky over Antelope Island and far from city lights, there was the Big Dipper, with the Milky Way absolutely clear and bright and awesome. Couples would lean over the railing above the salt sea beach and gaze upward. The stars were magnetic, magic, enveloping, and they almost lifted a person heavenward, no matter who his or her partner was!

Mood and memories are mixed up with place. And Saltair was unique in the lives of generations of couples.

Often we'd talk about how our dead sea was akin to the one in the Holy Land. Water flowed into it but not out of it. It was not a "giving lake." (How could it be a haven of romance with no giving?)

There is the river Jordan that connects our own freshwater, living lake located forty-five miles south (Utah Lake instead of Galilee) to the dead Great Salt Lake (instead of the Dead Sea). All of this brought Christ very close to us—right there in the rough, salty, sandy air in the shadow of Saltair's dance hall and fun house with its famed "mile-high" hardwood slide. And it all came together in a fine balance.

Saltair featured big-name bands for one night stands on a regular basis. To have the world come to Utah in those days was a big ego boost, for the dating community, at least.

"Imagine," we'd drawl, "in person! Glenn Miller!" Or Artie Shaw, Benny Goodman, The Dorseys, Shep Fields, Phil Harris. Jimmy Lunceford was a lesser light but our favorite long-stay fill-in orchestra. Swaying back and forth in front of the bandstand, we became friends with him through near nightly visits.

Saltair was the only musical training that some youth ever received in that era of hard times. We could hum the melody as well as the harmony of all the theme songs of the various bands. We knew the names of the drummers and horn soloists, the singers. One of our town girls even fell in love and married one of the famous male singers.

Take Eddie Howard, for example. We stared at him so hard, so long, and so often that we knew him better than our fathers. All the girls fell for him, and when he sang "To Each His Own" the silly ones squealed and swooned. The rest of us just swooned into the arms of whatever poor swain we were dating that night.

For the boys, the money to take a girl to Saltair was hard to come by. We're talking pre–World War II—depression. Gratitude was my most ardent feeling toward a boy who took me to Saltair back then, but if he could dance, all the better. Sometimes dancing was a kind of gymnastic experience. Certain boys pumped your arm like iron and pushed you relentlessly across that long, slick floor, as if they were managing a mowing machine. It wasn't romantic, of course, but it was all we had, and so all the while we'd murmur, "Hey, it's OK. It's OK. Just being at Saltair is what counts." And it was.

Maybe the best thing about Saltair was the open-air train that shuttled the resort patrons those nineteen miles from Eleventh West and North Temple to the Great Salt Lake. Midday it was a casual scenic trip with passengers noting the current water level on either side of the train.

Midnight was another matter.

It was after the dance.

It was dark.

It was cold, which had its own reward, however.

The train was boarded by means of steps that ran the full length of each car on both sides. That gave quick access to the rows of benches and created happy collisions and endless giggles as couples would crowd on a row from both sides. The benches flipped to face the direction the passengers wanted—facing each other, looking longingly back at the pavilion, or checking the proximity of the city ahead. Actually, few looked at anything anyway, because there was much huddling and snuggling on board. Desert temperatures often dropped as much as forty degrees at night, and breezes whipped across the salt flats adding a windchill factor.

This open-air train was no silver streak. It took more than an hour to get from one stop to the next. It was early morning before the dancers got back in town. Some parents were hard-pressed about whether to let their children risk going home in a private car driven by a "reckless youth" on a two-way road or to let them take the train with the windchill factor—and the snuggling.

The first time my parents allowed me to ride the train home with our crowd was memorable. We hadn't been under way long when I spotted my father scooting along the outside steps and peering anxiously down each row—for me, of course.

The sight of a real live parent on board after a dance, checking up, released a silent signal. En masse heads buried into shoulders, out of sight.

The next day I overheard my father explaining to my Mother, "No, I didn't find her. Yes, the kids *were* all wrapped up in each other, but I tell you it was harmless. An act of mercy, really. They were motivated by cold not lust."

"One thing leads to another," Mother mused.

"Well, don't ever make me do that again. I nearly froze to death. If you are so worried just keep her home. Saltair isn't worth it."

Mother looked lovingly at Dad, as she touched his arm with her special pat and crooned, "It was to me!"

And it was to me.

21

Words of Love

One of the clever touches in Shakespeare's *Two Gentlemen from Verona* is the use of small books of definitions that hang on long ribbons from the waists of each of the four lovers. The characters refer to their books of manners frequently during the play, to put words in their own mouths, to find words of love better than they might be able to think of themselves!

Some people are gifted at putting the essence of an emotion or a life experience into bright phrasing. Others of us plow or slither or tumble or romp through whatever happens to us. We are glad if someone can tell us where we have been and what we are feeling!

We turn now to some words of love used by lovers over the ages and recorded by some gifted scribes.

Careful, now! Some of these lines could have you melting. So much the better. The long, sweet song of love can stir up feelings that you might not know you have—or that you had forgotten. A life touched by love is softened for good purposes, you know. However, twenty-four hours a day of such heightened feeling might well be a little much. But for now and then, to psyche you into gentler behavior . . . why not? In fact . . . mmmm!

> Music I heard with you was more than music,
> And bread I broke with you was more than bread.
>
> —Conrad Aiken

> I don't stop to ask myself
> Do I love him? but
> laugh for joy.
>
> —Denise Levertov

Love You!

My heart is like a singing bird
Whose nest is in a watered shoot;
My heart is like an apple-tree
Whose boughs are bent with thick-set fruit.
My heart is gladder than all these
Because my love is come to me
Because the birthday of my life,
Is come, my love is come to me.

—Christina Rossetti

Christie Lund wrote the following lines at some sweet point in her own life. Wouldn't it be a satisfying credit to have said these words of love—to have felt that way, too?

Kissed before? My memory replies:
"A dozen times or more."
But my throbbing, singing heart denies:
"No, not ever . . . really . . . kissed before."

And now words of comfort to any old codger (male or female), but let budding young lovers take note of this excerpt from one of Shakespeare's sonnets:

Love's not Time's fool, though rosy lips and cheeks
Within his bending sickle's compass come;
Love alters not with his brief hours and weeks,
But bears it out even to the edge of doom.

22

Love—for In-Laws, Too?

Is there love after in-laws?

Has to be!

In-law is a legal classification. But it means people with whom we are related through marriage. Someone in our immediate family married somebody from another family and, lo and behold, we have legal relatives not of our own choosing and whom we are required by God to love.

A sister brings a brother-in-law into our life.

A son brings a daughter-in-law into the family.

Mother, being widowed or divorced, takes a second husband.

Choose a spouse and reap a houseful of people you may or may not know, have anything in common with, or even like, let alone love. At least in the beginning.

After the fact, however, down the road a piece and through the years, behaving in love toward God's other children is a requirement. Behavior can be trained or mentally prepared for, but ultimately behavior stems from the heart and mind. Behavior springs from a feeling. Learning to love in-laws requires certain feelings to insure certain behavior. Love is a feeling. Love is not passive. Relating to in-laws requires action of some kind, too. Behaving lovingly toward these extended family members happens more readily if the soul is prepared.

We walk over the bridges we build.

The proverbial bed we make we must then lie down upon.

Divorce is a legal action, too, but even in this case the relating, the interacting, goes on and on and on.

We can change a name, an address, a mate, but still we must interact with those who have once been tagged "family, in-laws, relatives."

We might just as well learn to interact in love, allowing ourselves to be prompted by authentic feelings of affection for others of God's family—to whom, by the way, we are closer than "in-law."

Why not build bridges that are comfortable and sure?

Why not develop habits of love and loyalty, patience and helpfulness, forgiveness and forbearance? Doing so is much easier than slogging through the mire only to find that a document doesn't alter relating, interacting, even legal responsibility. Add to that God's commandment to love all his children.

Living in love can be done. There are notable precedents.

The biblical book of Ruth is a classic example of the blessings that can come from living in love with in-laws. Each of the starring characters played his or her role appropriately, guided by love and loyalty. Ruth clave unto her mother-in-law after the death of her husband. Naomi loved and cared for her daughter-in-law Ruth. Boaz cared for Ruth, who was the widow of one of his relatives.

What can we learn from this story?

Ruth insisted to Naomi that she would go wherever Naomi went. She said, "Thy people shall be my people, and thy God my God." She loved enough to change. She was obedient and teachable. "All that thou sayest unto me I will do." She did not go empty to her mother-in-law but instead provided her with self-esteem and a reason to be needed, plus nourishment for her old age.

Boaz was not disgruntled about another mouth or two to feed! Nor about somebody else's mother-in-law moving in. He even went the second mile to see to personal comfort and well-being.

And Naomi helped. Counseled wisely. Was not a troublemaker when her dead son's wife married again. Loved the new grandchild as if it were her own.

In Book of Mormon history we learn of the relationship between the daughters of Ishmael and the sons of Lehi as they married and made a way in the wilderness together (1 Nephi 7). Times of rebellion in such a pilgrimage are inevitable among imperfect people. But there are ways of dealing with such uprisings—ways to bring peace and love. For example, when Nephi's brothers became violently angry and sought to take his life, some of his in-laws intervened. The scripture relates, "They were angry with me [Nephi] again, and sought to lay hands upon me; but behold, one of the daughters of Ishmael, yea, and also her mother, and one of the sons of Ishmael, did plead with my brethren, insomuch that they did soften their hearts; and they did cease striving to take away my life." In-laws saving the life of a man whose own brothers were trying to kill him. All right!

In Exodus 18 in the Bible we read the marvelous story of Jethro, who was father-in-law to Moses and was much concerned about him. The scripture says, "And Moses went out to meet his father in law, and did obeisance, and kissed him; and they asked each other of their welfare; and they came into the tent." The next day the two men talked over the problems of leadership. One had keen responsibility. The other shared his mature wisdom and advised Moses to follow the system of judges whereby to judge the people. And Moses "hearkened to the voice of his father in law, and did all that he had said."

We actually know little about the appearance, manner, likes, and dislikes of scriptural characters such as Ruth, Naomi, Nephi, Moses, Jethro. Perhaps they were appealing people—attractive, having pleasant personalities and unoffending mannerisms, easy to love and to live in love with. But perhaps they weren't attractive and loveable.

Nephi, Moses, and Ruth all had problems, and interacting with in-laws was on their agendas, too. We have problems and in-laws. We have commandments to live by, lives to build.

Tolerating isn't good enough. Love is required.

Now, since we are imperfect, different-from-each-other people who are required to live together in love—or interact in agony—it seems clear that applying Christlike principles to our life situations is a better pursuit than a caving in to the miserable ways of the world with its corps of counselors who might suggest a more selfish solution.

Here are three suggestions to consider from among Heavenly Father's many guides to help us reach the goal of living in love:

1. Continue in patience until we are perfected (see D&C 67:13).

2. Remember that we can do all things (even love our in-laws) through Christ who will strengthen us (see Philippians 4:13).

3. Begin to live according to his eternal law, irrevocably decreed before this earth was and upon which all blessings are predicated (see D&C 130:20).

We believe God lives. We believe he is our creator. We believe he is the author of the plan of life we are experiencing. If we are truly thoughtful we will realize that God knows the way we should travel and how we should cope with our challenges and how a disciple of his should behave.

Earth life is a training period. Good family relationships practiced here bring love, peace, and contentment, as well as help us qualify for exaltation as a member of an eternal family unit. Heaven just won't be heaven without love, and loving is learned on earth.

Heaven's Fire

A life in which love has surfaced is sweeter, more sanctified, and more satisfying. Exhilaration mingles with sacrifice and produces winged joy!

Love has been called "heaven's fire." It is like the sun shining over the whole earth—through love everything is seen in its best beauty. With love dictating the gentle, wondrous responses to God, nature, and all mankind, life has an awesome luster. It is amazing to realize that even unrequited love quickens the mind and flows back to soften the heart. True love ennobles.

But the withholding of love because of grief, envy, fatigue, self-pity, anger, lust, or sin is a mighty loss in life. It is to live as if Christ never lived and died for us. It is to deny ourselves the opportunity of drawing near enough to him to bask in his lifting spirit, to be inspired by his example, to be touched by his compassion.

"Bridle all your passions," Alma counseled his son Shiblon, "that ye may be filled with love" (Alma 38:12). There it is. When we have allowed our hearts to focus on negative emotions and self-defeating anxieties, we have no room for the workings of the Spirit. Only love and worship of Heavenly Father and Jesus Christ open our souls to the healing and peace that love brings. God is love, you see. The emotional upheaval of the adversary is not.

To love is to be closer to Christ—to match in our actions and thoughts the most profound and refining ideals of Deity. It is to be awakened to a pulsing compassion, a compelling awareness of all mankind. Finally, it is to feel the very real, grand expansion of the heart that spills into laughter, kindness, hope, and unending gratitude.

Love's Spell

A happy person is one who is full of love.

Love is the most used, misused, understood, misunderstood, simple yet profound word in our language. It is the most poignant, powerful, beautiful, fulfilling concept placed in the heart of man. Love is a thought given by God to man so that man might become like God.

Our capacity to love knows no bounds. We love each succeeding child as much as the one before. Incredible! We love life, nature, creatures, the land of our birth, ideas, causes, things, places, memories and dreams, aspirations, people—all kinds of people: old and young, parents and children, friends and foreigners, and that particular person who gives us unique satisfaction, a well-settled and complete feeling and purpose. And we do love God the Father, his Son, and the Holy Ghost.

Such is love's spell.

In the end we love best those things for which we have sacrificed and those dear ones whom we have served. It has been said that a life without love in it is like a heap of ashes upon a deserted hearth, the fire dead, the laughter stilled, the light extinguished. Ah, better to serve, to think of ways to give and stir up pleasure, to be busy casting love's spell among surprised associates. Marcus Aurelius Antoninus is credited with writing the advice, "Put yourself in harmony with the things among which your lot is cast; love those with whom you have your portion, with a true love."

Humble in spirit, kindly in deed, love judges tenderly, comforts in need!

Love's Plea

No one should be love-starved. But sadly, this happens in the "best" of families. Growing children need love, too.

> Says the little one:
> Touch me soft, be gentle
> Listen to me, care.
> Let me see your eyes so
> That I will *know* you're there.
>
> —Elaine Cannon

An unidentified author has written: "If you're ever going to love me love me now, while I can know all the sweet and tender feelings which from real affection flow. Love me now, while I am living; do not wait till I am gone and then chisel it in marble—warm love words on ice-cold stone. If you knew someone was thirsting for a drop of water sweet would you be so slow to bring it? Would you step with laggard feet? There are tender hearts all round us who are thirsting for our love; why withhold from them what nature makes them crave all else above?"

A child driven between divorced parents—each of whom required "visitation rights"—said, "I need somebody to love *me* and let me be a happy person. I feel like a lion in the circus with too many trainers, all with different whips, wanting me to do what they want me to do when they want me to do it."

Make love a living, working principle in life through daily acts of love in behalf of the Lord God and for the pleasantness of others. Pleasant—if life could be more pleasant! Then if the heart could be warmed sufficiently to satisfy for the day—or even the moment—we'd have taken a giant step toward making our heaven on earth.

> For we are members one of another. . . .
> Be ye kind one to another,
> tenderhearted,
> forgiving one another,
> even as God for Christ's sake hath forgiven you.
>
> —Ephesians 4:25, 32

Let us reject the hard and critical society of the cynic and follow the way of love. Softness is not weakness. Love protects children, eases the lot of women, ennobles men, welcomes strangers, helps the downtrodden, lifts up the hands that hang down, and straightens the bowed neck. As Pierre Teilhard de Chardin wrote, "Someday, after mastering the winds, the waves, the tides, and gravity, we shall harness for God the energies of love, and then for the second time in the history of the world, man will discover fire."

Indeed someday, after coping with computers, subduing satellites, mastering missiles, we will look to freedom, cleanness, education, healthfulness, removal of anxiety and gather together the processes that encourage human dignity and remind us that we are all God's beloved children; then we will more clearly see that the worth of souls is great in God's eyes and therefore should be in ours.

A Sonnet

Shakespeare should stand alone so that the exquisite expression of romantic love's power will not be missed. But not to romantic love alone does his message apply. Surely the situation and the words could just as well be those of a grateful friend, a work-weary husband, a devoted wife, a current disciple for an eternal Christ.

> When, in disgrace with Fortune and men's eyes,
> I all alone beweep my outcast state,
> And trouble deaf heaven with my bootless cries,
> And look upon myself and curse my fate,
> Wishing me like to one more rich in hope,
> Featured like him, like him with friends possessed,
> Desiring this man's art, and that man's scope,
> With what I most enjoy contented least;
> Yet in these thoughts myself almost despising,
> Haply I think on thee, and then my state,
> Like to the lark at break of day arising
> From sullen earth, sings hymns at heaven's gate;
>> *For thy sweet love rememb'red such wealth brings*
>> *That then I scorn to change my state with kings.*

Sentimental Truth

When love comes to some, there often follows a thrashing about among the works of the poets and the scribes to find words to express the magnificent feeling—to find the classic lines or obscure phrases that confirm one's feelings, describe one's ecstasy, eloquently confirm that the swelling of the heart is heaven-sent, that the tender turmoil in the mind marks the wondrous beginning of love.

Sometimes, in the soul's dry season, one just happens on a passage that lifts the spirit—like the ripples of wind through an umbrella willow or the rise and fall of a young girl's hair when a breeze passes by. Then love is remembered and is as healing and quickening as it is at its fresh height. It is then we feel what some staid folks might call mere sentimentality. But to the rest of us it is sacred truth. What we read of love can be a blessing.

Just for example, Rainer Maria Rilke wrote: "How can I hinder or restrain my soul so that it does not yearn for yours? . . . You and I are like a bow that's bound, though with two strings, to give a single sound. . . . O long, sweet song!"

Thomas Hardy described a sentimental truth: "Their eyes met. Measurement of life should be proportioned rather to the intensity of the experience than to its actual length. Their glance, but a moment chronologically, was a season in their history."

28

Precious Bane

Mary Webb's inimitable love story *Precious Bane,* first published in 1924, takes place in Shropshire, England, in early times, when feelings came from deep inner roots and not from media impact. It is about Prue Sarn, the lovely young girl who holds no personal hope for romance in life, because she has an ugly harelip. Yet she is one who can feel the love and hate of others flow about her without a word spoken.

Prue goes each year to the pond at the time of the troubling of the waters to watch the dragonflies struggle to "come out of their bodies" transformed! And the symbolism indicates that love can transform us all if only we can love enough. The scene of the beginning of Prue's love is a gathering of the village women, who meet together to spin thread.

> 'He brought me to His Lordly House,
> His Banner it was Love.'

And just as we were singing that, and the wheels going like churn-owls, there was a quick footfall without, and a rush of fresh air, and a long ray of sunshine from the door to me, and he stood there in the light looking upon us.

'He,' I say, as if you'd know him out of the world as I did.

He stood in the doorway, and I rose up from my seat in the shadows at the back of the room, as if he was my own bidden guest.

How did he look? What like was he? Was he well-favoured? It be hard to say. There are no looks in love, no outward seeming, no telling over of features. When you are but a moth in the candle of his eye, can you tell his stature, or if he be dark or fair? Did Magdalene . . . know, when she lay at the feet of the only man she ever loved yet never loved, whether the carpenter's Son featured His mother or not, whether He was big or little in stature? Shall we know, when we be come into His presence that made us, what outward seeming His majesty has? No. Only our hearts will tremble in the light.[5]

In the end, after many brave adventures, Weaver, Prue's love, saves her from torture by uneducated, prejudiced villagers. He scoops her into his arms and lifts her onto his horse, just like in her dream, and, we read, "the noise of the people sank away. . . . All sank, all faded in the quiet air." But Prue protests:

'But no! . . . You mun marry a girl like a lily. See, I be hare-shotten!'

But he wouldna listen. He wouldna argufy. Only after I'd pleaded agen myself a long while, he pulled up sharp, and looking down into my eyes, he said—

'No more sad talk! I've chosen my bit of Paradise. 'Tis on your breast, my dear acquaintance!'

And when he'd said those words, he bent his comely head and kissed me full upon the mouth.[6]

29

A Bond of Love

If one reads, heeds, gathers, and practices the many counsels about love, the heart becomes mellow, at last. The marketplace loses its appeal in favor of delight in another human being—or a family of them. For the bond of love is essentially the same, whether it is directed toward God, family, a particular person, or a significant stranger who touched your life in some way.

And while much of love's definition, qualities, and possibilities has been said before, consider again the sage and sweet things included here. For example, these lines from Gibran's *The Prophet:*

Love one another, but make not a bond of love:
Let it rather be a moving sea between the shores of your souls.
Fill each other's cup but drink not from one cup.
Give one another of your bread but eat not from the same loaf.
Sing and dance together and be joyous, but let each one of
    you be alone,
Even as the strings of a lute are alone though they quiver with
    the same music.[7]

The idea of being apart/together, two but one as lovers, as counseled in Gibran's poem, is reminiscent of Anne M. Lindbergh's description of dancers moving together to the same rhythm but facing different directions as they whirl and turn.[8] Two become "one flesh" under legal, lovely, and God-blessed circumstances, but each remains—in gender, spirit, character, gifts and *some* goals—a thing unique and separate.

And now these thoughts from David Cory, who suggests that love is more poignant, more remarkable, a sweeter agony than anything else:

Miss you, miss you, miss you;
Everything I do
Echoes with the laughter
And the voice of You.
You're on every corner,
Every turn and twist,
Every old familiar spot
Whispers how you're missed.
. . . .
Miss you, miss you, miss you!
Nothing now seems true

Only that 'twas heaven
Just to be with You.[9]

And these lines, from Carol Haynes's poem "Any Wife or Husband," show us a way to help keep the bond happy, better at the end than even at the beginning:

Let us be guests in one another's house
With deferential "No" and courteous "Yes";
Let us take care to hide our foolish moods
Behind a certain show of cheerfulness.

. . . .

Let us knock gently at each other's heart,
Glad of a chance to look within—and yet
Let us remember that to force one's way
Is the unpardoned breach of etiquette.[10]

Indeed!

Have you read lately "Jenny Kissed Me" by Leigh Hunt? If you have, was it for a school assignment, or did you find it browsing through an anthology? Did you encounter it in a yearbook entry or discover it on a folded paper tucked in your stocking drawer? Never mind; how or where isn't so important as reading it again for whatever reason. It expresses the exuberance of spontaneous love and the magic such love creates.

Jenny kissed me when we met,
 Jumping from the chair she sat in.
Time, you thief! who love to get
 Sweets into your list, put that in.
Say I'm weary, say I'm sad;
 Say that health and wealth have missed me;
Say I'm growing old, but add—
 Jenny kissed me![11]

30

Love and Marriage

"And how do you think you've gained all this weight?" the diet-center counselor asked the client.

"I love my family so much—"

"Ah, yes. You are one of those cook-them-into-heaven women."

"No. Actually, I'm a terrible cook. But I make a great stack of toast in the morning. When I've buttered and jellied each slice I take a love bite out of it. We have seven children, and my husband is a toast man. That counts up to a lot of bites each day, I guess."

There are many ways of feeling love in marriage.

There was the woman who for thirty-seven years nagged at her husband to pick up his soiled socks from the floor near the bedpost where he dropped them each night. Nothing changed, until he died, that is. Then she grieved and grieved and would have given, as she said, "a favorite Lladro" to see those socks tumbled on the floor and his tousled head resting on the pillow.

Now she wants to make speeches at wedding receptions of the very young and tell them all the things nobody told her, all that she didn't learn until it was too late.

Always remember and never forget that the human soul is tender and that God considers every one of us worthwhile and precious. So who do we think we are that we can gripe about soiled socks, capless toothpaste, overdrafts, spitting-snuffing-snoring, women with nonstop tongues, and on ad nauseam?

One couple I know keeps peace by communicating with memos —office style. No need to write a life story, they say, it's all there in the duplicate copies. Well, whatever sails your ship!

The hard work of communication in a marriage takes ongoing time and attention. People change. Stress cuts in. Wave lengths shift. There is seldom time to lay a base of understanding, to pave the way to get your way, as the saying goes. But the bottom line is, as we say at our house, "Would you rather be right or loved?"

Remember, you have your free agency to toss married love in the out bin, if being right every time is of prime importance to you.

"It's only money"—indeed, there is no money in heaven. "It's a mere trifle"—exactly, for what's a kaput water heater and a flooded basement in the eternal scheme of things?

An attitude of gratitude, a demeanor of humility, an aura of love about you require commitment to quality years of closeness. Nothing else will do. Living a life of quiet desperation may give you credit for not ruining the children's concept of which father to obey, but surely points for being Christlike are not earned in such a home. And taking cakes to the funeral supper doesn't count. Heaven's happiness has to begin at home.

Healthy relationships grow out of couples who know who they are, what they want from the whole scope of life. Such couples are responsible not only for their partner's possibility of joy but also for their own vulnerability. Happy relationships are rooted in reality, not movie plots. God has told us how to achieve relationships of this type. Prophets have reminded. Psychologists are getting online, too. It takes two to lie in lovely love and the same two to walk the strait path together, heads erect and hearts full of faith, hope, and charity.

In her diary Anne M. Lindbergh records:

Charles comes home. I am just leaving the trailer when I see him, lanky blue figure tumbling down the hill from the house to find me.

It is so strange to see someone like that, whom you love, suddenly coming down the steps in all his warm bodily reality, to catch sight of him before he sees you, and to feel suddenly, in one of those incredible flashes of vision in life: "How much he means to me—all of life is coming down the steps to me."

And then the vision goes with physical closeness, with the familiar "coming home" to one's husband.[12]

Will Durant said that there really can't be any lasting happiness without love. There can be no fulfillment of life's ultimate purpose without a successful marriage and a good family life. While this is true, we can also thank goodness for good Church support, meaningful programs and relationships, and inspired understanding for the many single people abroad in the land!

Anyway, perhaps the greatest blessing in marriage is when it lasts long and the couple grows with changing interests, branching out in assignment, pursuit of talent, and coming back to share the learning. Impermanent relationships do not provide the hard-won joys that deepen between two people who have watched each other grow up.

Till Death Do Us Part

Love may be sweeter in the end than in the beginning.

The first part of any relationship has a certain purity, an exciting self-consciousness in the company of that one loved. New friendship, new love is simple and straightforward for a time. Where it goes from there—how that bud blooms and flowers out—is part of the keen interest we all take in the experience.

Love among friends is easy at first. One of life's choice rewards. Different from school-day relationships, adult friendship meets needs—needs that might not fully be met if we put all our expectations into the lap of a spouse. Doing so would result in an impossible prospect for total fulfillment, so there is a welcoming to other (yes, appropriate) relationships from which honey can be gathered and brought back to the hive—and spouse. Professional connections, church relationships that come with assignments, neighbors, golf buddies, or craft-class companions are some possibilities.

Beyond that, there are social groups that become increasingly important as the years whiz by. "Friends and loved ones," we call them in our precious circles.

And yet . . . at the end of the line there is such helplessness to appropriately express love. And love does need to be expressed all along the way for the sake of both parties.

A crash, a death, a swift separation without preparation. Those left behind are startled as well as sad. Often they are stricken with frustration, because so much is left undone, unsaid. They race to fill in blanks and say to each other what never got shared with the deceased.

A stroke victim is another matter. He receives the blooming plant, the get-well cards. He doesn't die, so loved ones move on with their lives while he slowly begins his lonely, often prolonged descent to death. Burdened with an unfamiliar body, wonders, "Who am I? Now—who am I?" The victim suffers a crippling of sacred emotion that is less visible than the physical damage, but more hurtful. Friends see him but don't know what to say, how to treat him. He is changed, and there isn't time anymore for people to learn to love him again.

With the terminally ill, friends reach out, loved ones agonize and rally round. The luxury of knowing death's time allows for getting one's affairs in order—romantic attachments, family members, professional colleagues can be thanked, paid tribute, bid a tearful farewell. There can come peace in an exchange of love and gratitude.

Other precious moments can be programmed in. Consider the case of a dying United States senator who was guided by an Apostle of the Lord God into a courageous understanding of his rights. Like Jacob of old, the senator gave each of his children a father's blessing. In death the love was stronger between them than ever in life. And hope for the eternal future was a reality.

A young man was drafted and assigned to the air force. He lived in the country and his father made special arrangements to drive the boy to the depot to board the bus to the induction center. The baggage was loaded, ticket taken, and suddenly the father awkwardly wrapped his arms around his son, hugging and kissing him. He wept as his son left.

The draftee was stunned. He'd never had such affection shown him by his father—ever. The bus ride was dismal. The young man was certain it was because he'd never see his father again. He thought, "My father would never have done what he did if he had not been certain that I was going to be killed."

The long years without loving exchange between father and son had distorted the son's thinking.

Later the young man read a letter that his father had written that same day to a sister. In it the father confessed that only the day before the son's departure for military service had he been told that he only had six months to live. They'd never see each other again, but it would be because the father was terminally ill. He asked the sister to share the letter after his death. He wanted the son to know how much he loved him, valued him as a human being, enjoyed him as a son.

Better late than never. Though death part us, survival in affectionate memory can assuage grief. But if only . . .

The young man learned an important lesson from that experience. A person should frequently, sincerely, unfailingly tell family and friends how much they are loved![13]

President David O. McKay once said, "Always remember that the human heart is tender, and each individual is precious to our Heavenly Father."

A person loves as he can, as he has learned by example and experience. We must accept love how and when it comes and not spoil it by judgment or regret. Still, it is good to learn and to improve and thus help the mass of humanity to inch forward in making life more pleasant—even more wonderful, perhaps.

Careful Love

One of life's finest offerings is true affection and affinity between two people. Finding—happening onto—another human being whose chemistry responds to yours, permitting an ever-increasing, inner aura of love between you, is a wonder. Sir Hugh Walpole once described this miracle as "a sort of divine accident." You don't get it by going forth and passionately pursuing it.

Predestined . . . foreordained . . . lucky . . . blessed . . . coincidence? Whatever. Love is lovely. Friendship is fulfilling and a soothing salve for skinned knees taken along life's trail.

Such a blessing requires careful handling.

Emerson spoke of walking in the morning with "a profound gratitude"—for his friends. Some have gone to sleep feeling that way. Victor Hugo spoke the truth when he reported that a lifelong nourishment of relationships is worth the effort. He wrote, "Winter is on my head; spring is in my heart." Keeps you young, sharing warm feelings for others—especially one particular other.

Two persons who love each other are in a place more holy than the interior of a church, one sage pronounced. Good imagery, which leads us into another aspect of careful love: *what love withholds in love.*

Can we get away with such thoughts in today's "do-your-own-thing-no-matter-what" syndrome? Let's see.

Remember *Camelot*—that romantic, dazzling musical with knights in shining armor, high ideals, the good King Arthur, his young wife Guenevere, and the noble Lancelot, whose "honor was his strength"? And it is a story filled with tragedy, too. Remember the song sung by Lancelot and Guenevere as they have become lovers and now recognize the terrible truth about love-out-of-bounds? The lesson the lyrics teach is that suffering love in restraint and in silence is one thing; but when self-control is abandoned and selfishness pursued with stolen moments of love, there is worse suffering. Guenevere concludes the song with these words:

> And after all had been said,
> Here we are, my love,
> Silent once more
> And not far, my love . . .
> From where we were *before.*[14]

Oh, careful love is better!

It was a delight to listen to poet Paul Engle lecture on a personal appearance tour to western colleges. He read some of his own poetry including, these lines: "Finding you, unexpectedly, in that room / Was more than a mere person in love could stand, / As if on a summer day in the dazzle of noon / One snowflake fell on my astonished hand."

The classic case of careful love, of restraint against love-out-of-bounds, concerns Joseph who was sold into slavery in Egypt. Having worked his way up the palace ladder, he was sorely tempted on repeated occasions by Potiphar's wife. His valor in resisting her allurements is a choice example of personal purity. You recall the incident recorded in Genesis 39: "And she caught him by his garment, saying, Lie with me: and he left his garment in her hand, and fled, and got him out." Her false accusations and his imprisonment and discomfort notwithstanding, Joseph was valiant. His protection was his faith—"How then can I do this great wickedness, and sin against God?"

And now this important message, by an unidentified author, that should be taught to every young lover, every frustrated friend, every God-loving disciple who cares more about others than self!

> There is a giving beyond giving
> > Yours to me
> > Who awoke last night
> > Hours before the dawn
> > Set free

By one intolerable lightning stroke
That ripped the sky—
To understand what love withholds in love
And why.

Maybe we can't help falling in love, but we *can* help what we do about it. We need to be very, very careful, for a lot of reasons.

Love as God Loves

Emerson's essay on friendship has been the classic statement on the precious quality of relationships. He writes such thought-provoking phrases as, "The heart has its Sabbath and jubilees," and "Love is our highest work and the synonym of God."

It is admirable to be capable of steady friendship, to care enough about other human beings that we experience their suffering with them—loving them the more because we can do nothing to alleviate their pain or eliminate their problems. When they weep we taste salt.

The love of God assures us of the purpose of life. He knows of our crises and our deepest cares. Not always will he eliminate our trials at the moment. But he will love, support, sustain, and supply us with hope that all things will work to our good. We are not forgotten by him. He takes our burdens on his back. He weeps with us, so to speak, and does not leave us alone in our trials.

As we learn to support our friends in such a way, we can say that we love as God loves. We are not only followers after him; we are also becoming ever more like him.

34

Ebb and Flow

Relationships come and relationships go. Even very close relationships. This is true on every level of life and with most people.

Children trade best friends like baseball cards.

Old men play golf regularly with other old men who can still play golf. And count them close friends—as long as they can still play golf.

A well-to-do old woman gave her oriental rugs to a neighbor who was close by instead of a daughter who was far away. The woman was getting her life in order. She was getting close to crossing the proverbial bar and she knew it. The neighbor knew it, too, and cradled the old lady in love.

A young wife draws close to the friend who is a good listener. This friend seems to have a *guarded heart.* The relationship flows. But if the friend tells, if she talks, the friendship is violated. It ebbs.

A marriage between two imperfect but intelligent people can grow in importance, meaning, and permanence. Takes effort, of course. It takes understanding of the fact that relationships change—even the best of them. They ebb and flow, affected by a variety of happenings typical of family life and personal struggle.

And that isn't all bad. It keeps life interesting. It marks growth.

There is a sure impact made on a marriage during times of moving, serving, working out of the home, illness, natural interaction with other attractive people. It is vital to get one's priorities straight. "Control thyself!" is the chant for the greater good of all concerned.

It has been said that the things that matter most must not be at the expense of the things that matter least. Children, extended-family members, the investment of time and energy and money, personal reputation are all in jeopardy.

Evaluate your expectations carefully, candidly, hmmm?

Anne Morrow Lindbergh touches the right heart chord in this quote from her book *Gift from the Sea:* "When you love someone you do not love them all the time, in exactly the same way, from moment to moment. It is an impossibility. It is even a lie to pretend to. And yet this is exactly what most of us demand. We have so little faith in the ebb and flow of life, of love, of relationships. We leap at the flow of the tide and resist in terror its ebb. We are afraid it will never return. . . . The only real security is not in owning or possessing, not in demanding or expecting, not in hoping, even. Security in a relationship lies neither in looking back to what it was in nostalgia, nor forward to what it might be in dread or anticipation, but living in the present relationship and accepting it as it is now."[15]

And, it might be added, accepting it with great gratitude to God, all the while asking for his help, for his blessing to help you two protect, revere, and enhance your alliance.

Love without Marriage

Each lived alone in the same condo complex. A hall separated their individual entrances, but they had keys to each other's door. They were welcome in each other's home.

He was by her side for as much time as the hospital would permit when she underwent critical surgery. She made him little meals and special treats when she was well. He fixed her garage door opener. She ironed his dress shirts. He received her UPS deliveries.

She signed for his Federal Express mail. He zipped up her dinner gown. She tied his bow tie. She massaged his shoulders, stressed from crunching over a computer. He provided reflex treatment for her feet, sore from standing to bottle Hale peaches, freeze berries, prepare pickles.

They worked a small garden plot together, harvesting the fruit and vegetables in season. They listened to each other's views after the six o'clock news and a predinner refreshment.

Grocery shopping was a joint affair—separate baskets and receipts at the checkout, but she advised and suggested, and he lifted the heavies. They took meals at her condo and read to each other in his because he had the most comfortable chairs, side by side. They read poetry and lines from a variety of books—an eclectic list including the scriptures, Ariel and Will Durant, Morris West's novels, A. E. Housman, Walt Whitman, Norman Cousins, Arrington, Chaim Potok, and the latest how-to book on the best-seller list. And they subscribed to the Sunday *New York Times* just for the book review section, which they considered next to the scriptures for guidance.

Their embraces were long and warm, full of deep sighs, cheek stroking, ear tickling. No inappropriate intimacy, just a ripple of fingers to each other through the closing doors. It was a years-old signal that meant something special to them. Peace, dear friend! . . . Sleep well . . . Dream of me . . . God bless . . . Mizpah . . . Take care . . . *Love you!*

A perfect relationship. He was a widower, she a widow. They were devoted friends. He was eighty-two and she was eighty-three.

It was true love, but without marriage, and it lasted for twenty-five years!

36

Love among Little Ones

It had been a lively birthday party. Now the refreshments were over and the children had moved to the play areas of the house while the adults visited in the living room before departure.

Suddenly—like God on High noting the pathetic and sometimes dangerous mistakes of growing mankind—suddenly we noticed a two-year-old in a frightening situation.

The chocolate birthday cake on the pedestal cake platter standing unguarded on the dining table was too much of a temptation to resist. The child reached up high and found the long, sharp cutting knife and attacked the cake. Aunt Kathy gasped and raced to the scene. Everyone watched while she carefully but firmly took the knife from the protesting child. Oh, he was angry! He was disappointed and deprived. He lashed out with both hands to hit the aunt again and again and again. She tried to calm him, soothing him with simple explanation. She offered him a piece of cake she cut—to no avail.

The tantrum lasted while the adults moved toward the front hall to leave—still visiting as loved ones do. Then Jon, in his swinging toddler gait, pressed through the gathered relatives to seek Aunt Kathy. This time he stood still in front of her and thrust his hand toward her. He opened his pudgy palm to reveal a birthday candle, and he held it there until she took his child-gift. Then he smiled.

Amazing! Wonderful! Here was ''sin'' and anger, repentance and forgiveness, and an outpouring of love for a healing.

The adults were startled at this rehearsal of the basics in human relationships being enacted by a two-year-old. The little child did teach them. All was well.

Amy's baby-sitter, who had tended Amy for all of her three years, was being married. Amy thought this called for a special gift —her own creation, of course. Busily she searched for supplies in mother's sewing basket, the junk drawer, and the jewelry sack of the costume box. That night at the reception Amy left her parents' side to run to the bride with her package—not the neatest-looking wrap job ever produced, but a gift given in sheer delight. The bride took her attention from the line of grown-up guests and carefully unwrapped the gift before the excited child. Sequins, straight pins, styrofoam ball, bag-top twisters wound together and poked into the ball.

"Oh!" exclaimed Susan. "Thank you for this . . . uh . . ."

"It's a bride's ring!" explained Amy, who knew that girls getting married had rings, because she had even tried Susan's on during a baby-tending session.

Spontaneous applause broke out among the wedding guests. It was a gift from the heart, an offering of self—child-executed but love-motivated.

Loving Relations

Strangers often exchange more personal information with their seat partner on an airplane than they would share with friends. Such was the case with the wealthy owner of a wine company.

When he learned that his seat companion was a woman deeply involved with youth, he told a significant story about love and children.

He was the oldest of five children, and not very old at that, when his mother died at the birth of his youngest sister. The father, who started the successful wine company when he emigrated from Italy, made temporary arrangements for the children and went back to Italy to "find a proper Italian woman" to mother his brood. He met, courted, and married a schoolteacher who had never been married and whose only experience with children was in the organized setting of a classroom. Cooking, cleaning, mending, mothering were not her forte, but he brought her back to America and her formal schooling in family life quickly began. There were a couple of new babies added to the family circle, as well.

The husband left her to her duties and went on about his business of traveling coast to coast to prosper his wine company.

Then suddenly, it seemed, the children grew up and had families of their own. It was time to celebrate twenty-five years of marriage for the older couple.

"At the big family dinner I looked over at my mother—stepmother to be exact—and felt a swift surge of wonder and love for her. How had she done it? How had she made us all feel as loved and accepted as if we were her very own? I was having trouble with my own teenagers, and I wanted to know her secret."

The man wiped a tear before he continued telling his story to his traveling companion. Then he became quite emotional, with tears filling his eyes, and he reached for his linen handkerchief, his jeweled cuff links flashing.

"I walked over to her, put my arm around her shoulder, and kissed the top of her head. I asked for her secret with children —with children not her own, really.

"She said, 'Oh, son! I loved your father and so I loved his children.' "

If we love the Father we can learn to love his children.

President George Q. Cannon and his brother Angus lived in Salt Lake City during the time of polygamy. One day they were walking down the street in front of the old Zion's Cooperative Mercantile Institution. A familiar-looking youth approached them.

"Is that one of your boys, Angus?" asked President Cannon.

"No, George, I think that's one of yours!"

But they both hugged the boy when he reached them.

Theirs was a big family, with the blending of many other family lines, thanks to wives. But the children ran in and out of all the houses and were comforted or disciplined by whomever as needed.

And love was there.

In an issue of *Reader's Digest* this story appeared over the initials S. W. R.:

> My Aunt Ruby and Uncle Arnie, childless after five years of marriage, jumped at the chance to adopt a baby boy. A short time later, Aunt Ruby became pregnant and gave birth to a boy.
>
> I was visiting one day when the kids were about eight and nine. A woman in our small community came to call. "Which boy is yours, Ruby?" she asked, observing the kids at play.
>
> "Both of them," my aunt replied.
>
> The caller persisted. "But I mean, which one is adopted?"
>
> Aunt Ruby did not hesitate. In her finest hour, she looked straight at her guest and replied, "I've forgotten!"[16]

The twelve-year-old was being ordained to the Aaronic Priesthood. In the circle, with their hands on his head, were his father and his father's father, his father's brothers and brother-in-law, and "Grandpa Jacobsen," the father of his father's first wife (she was now deceased and his own mother was the second wife).

It was a circle of love. Grandpa Jacobsen knew no difference between this boy and the children of his children. Affection, assistance, respect, and love were genuine.

Tender spirits thrive and reach out to others in a much broader context under such circumstances. The vision of an eternal family reaching across many generations and many varying relationships is possible.

In the Ziegler family business newsletter, which comes each month from Atlanta, Georgia, the following touching story appeared. It is used here with permission.

A woman at a gathering was so serene and lovely to look at that an older lady was surprised to learn she was the mother of seven young children. When two of the children entered the room, both about the same height, the older woman remarked that it must have been hard having them so close together.

"Not at all," the mother said. "We adopted Debbie three years ago."

"Good heavens!" the other burst out. "Didn't you have enough of your own?"

"Yes, of course," was the quick reply, "but Debbie had no one at all."

And that reminds me that one Halloween a chic young mother of many showed up at our door with two additional children. Her six-year-old we recognized, in spite of his Heisman Trophy candidate costume; but we questioned the identity of a five-year-old pink bunny and a seven-year-old princess.

"These are our two new daughters," the mother explained.

"We're adopted!" chirped the princess happily. And they took their treats and escaped from the door.

The mother lingered long enough for me to whisper, "Surely you don't *need* any more children!"

"No, we don't *need* any more children, but they needed us!"

38

Ex-Love

When Jeremy and Tricia were divorced it was heartbreak all around—heartbreak for everyone but Tricia. She had fallen in love with someone else, and she couldn't think of anything except being with him.

She couldn't think of Jeremy.

She couldn't think of their four children, either.

And she didn't even try to think about Jeremy's widowed mother. It just never occurred to her.

That's where Tricia made her mistake. Jeremy's mother knew about loving, and she was undaunted in her plans to keep heaven —and those grandchildren—as part of her family life.

Heaven is synonymous with love, not hate. That meant that the inevitable hurt accompanying divorce must be assuaged. Tricia had to have her way, but love could work miracles in the realignment of relationships. One's ex-love *could* at least become one's friend.

Jeremy's mother put the gospel into action. Understanding, patience, affectionate hugs, phone calls, tot tending were practical approaches. Constant prayers for guidance and good ideas, for a loving spirit and the softening of hearts were ever part of her agenda.

When it was Jeremy's turn to have the children for Thanksgiving, Tricia's new husband received a personal invitation to bring her to the big feast, too. Christmas Eve at Grandma's had always been a beloved tradition. Tricia and her new love were urged to come "for the sake of the children." And at last they came. It was awkward at first, and Jeremy had to be prodded a bit, too, "for the sake of the children."

It became a tradition for this new "family" to be together on Christmas Eve.

After a while everyone settled down into one big family who showed up at the school events, the baptisms, the hospital bedside, the soccer games. The former husband and wife were still parents and acted like it until they became healed in friendship.

Jeremy married again, too, after many long years. He's brought a wife and two grown-up children into this ever-enlarging family circle. No threats. No remembered hurts. Just nice people accommodating each other's behavior after the manner of Christ—as much as possible when people aren't perfect!

Ex-love? *New* love! And why not? Life is too important for anything less.

Loving Anyway

The cartoon shows two old human beings—their bodies are worn but their hearts are mellow; the mind is quick but the timing is off; the spirit is willing but the flesh is weak. They sit, each in a rocker, as she holds an earphone to her ear for better reception of the song he plays on the recorder he holds.

The music? "I'll See You in My Dreams!"

Have you heard about the nervous wife who said to her husband, "Darling, will you love me when I am old and ugly?"

He quickly replied, "Dearie, I do! I do! I do!"

As God Loves You

Sometimes we go pell-mell along, following our own will, forgetting that God's wisdom and will for us are wiser than our own.

Being impatient reflects a certain headstrong attitude, an arrogance that suggests we might know more than God (or the prophet or a loving parent).

Chi was that way when she joined the Church. She didn't prepare her family for the changes that would come into her life. She just wanted to be part of the activities of the great church she had become acquainted with through the young missionaries. Her parents didn't understand why. When Chi was baptized her parents allowed her to still live at home, but they didn't speak to her at all. If any communication was absolutely necessary a note was pinned to her pillow. At meals, through household chores and life's demands, it was as if Chi didn't exist. She'd come home from school every afternoon, and no one was allowed to speak to her. A silent house. A house of hurt.

Chi prayed a lot about this. She studied her scriptures. She finally made an appointment to talk the problem over with her priesthood leader.

"God is love, Chi. Try to love your parents as God loves you. You've shared with us how you have felt his love through all this time. Surely your parents are hurting, too, to take such drastic steps. See if you can duplicate God's love for you as you love your parents."

So Chi counted her blessings; she remembered God's goodness to her. Then she began showing forth her own kind of goodness and kindness to her parents. More work around the house. Surprises on their pillows. A hug from behind. Many smiles. A favorite dish prepared for dinner. A letter in the mail describing her love for them or congratulating them on some honor. A beautiful card on which she listed some of the many blessings she enjoyed because of her parents.

Then Chi became ill. Mother held Chi's hand and gave her careful nursing care. But she still didn't talk to Chi. One night, when Chi's condition worsened, she weakly asked her mother and father to kneel by her bed and pray for her. They did this and arose weeping, softened and grateful to have such a lovely daughter—even if some of her ideas were strange to them. They were enveloped in love, and it was a healing of heart and body for Chi.

41

In the Name of Love

Smith's wife was dying. There wasn't much time left. Threatened with separation, he realized how much he loved her. There was something he had to do about it before it was too late. It would be tough—so tough—but he knew he had to do it.

He said a kind of prayer for strength and then called the bishop for an appointment.

The grieving young husband and the equally young bishop faced each other across the desk and discussed the promise that life once held for the Smiths. What Smith wanted was a recommend so that he could take the woman he loved to the temple to be married for time and all eternity.

There were problems with this good idea. There was so little time, and Smith did not keep the Word of Wisdom. It had been a stumbling block to him for many years. However, he loved his wife and he would do anything . . .

"Anything?" the young bishop asked.

"Anything!" the desperate husband replied.

"Promise me you'll never break the Word of Wisdom again. Never."

The two talked about this at some length before a decision was reached. But then, the bishop was compassionate. Incredible! Overwhelmed, Smith gave his solemn word that addictive substances would somehow be held in control.

The two shook hands and on the strength of the promise, proper arrangements were made for the sacred temple experience. Smith left with a heart full of hope and gratitude for this unusual kindness from the bishop.

It was done. There was joy for a brief period, and then the young wife died. Bishop Jim moved his family from the neighborhood and people went on with their lives. Forty years passed before these two men locked hearts again.

Smith finally tracked down his former bishop and made an appointment. They were older men now. Jim was a stroke victim, with a walker and wheelchair as part of his life-style. His life as a bishop seemed forever ago and he had almost forgotten Smith; he couldn't imagine why he would want an appointment at this late date.

Smith, on the other hand, was terminally ill and didn't have much longer to live on earth. He determined to get his life in order—again. This time he came in love. Smith wanted his former bishop to know that for all these many years he had kept his word. He had never broken the Word of Wisdom.

Smith said that at first he'd felt only deep gratitude toward Bishop Jim in the months that followed their first meeting and handshake. But as the months and years followed, understanding increased. Then love mingled with gratitude. Love for a good friend and religious leader. Love for God and the plan of life.

The temple experience had comforted Smith after his wife's death, but it had also directed him for all the rest of his life. He was a changed man.

Now as time was short, Smith came to Jim in the name of love. Jim, who had been a compassionate bishop who truly cared about his flock more than mere rules, deserved to know the details.

"I've kept my word to you all these years," confessed Smith. He died soon after this visit.

Relationships marked with love make all the difference.

Civil Love, Sacred Love

Love lasts. Love between two people can reach beyond them to soften the lives of others. Regardless of the century or the situation, the romances of classic couples still enchant us. Consider Abigail and John Adams, Abelard and Heloise, Anthony and Cleopatra, Romeo and Juliet, Heber and Vilate Kimball, David and Emma Rae McKay.

And now Americans are touched by another loving couple whose civil love, sacred love spreads past their own hearts to stir up love in others.

Over a hundred years ago a thirty-four-year-old Major Sullivan Ballou of Rhode Island was mortally wounded in the Battle of Bull Run. The episode went unnoticed except by those closest to him — the battle was but one of many bloody events taking the lives of shocking numbers of soldiers in the Civil War.

Today Sullivan is discovered to be not only a hero who rides to his death leading his forces into battle but also a sensitive man with a gift for loving and expressing that rare love. A week before the fateful battle, he felt impelled to write a letter to his wife that might, he said, "fall under your eye when I shall be no more."

That letter was read to America as part of the stunning PBS television documentary *The Civil War.* It made America weep. It made Sullivan live again in the hearts of people who yearn to feel such love themselves and to be able to express it as eloquently as did this officer and gentleman. The poignant letter read, in part:

My dear Sarah, never forget how much I love you, and when my last breath escapes me on the battlefield, it will whisper your name. . . .

But, O Sarah! If the dead can come back to this earth and flit unseen around those they loved, I shall always be near you . . . always, always, and if there be a soft breeze upon your cheek, it shall be my breath, as the cool air fans your throbbing temple, it shall be my spirit passing by. Sarah, do not mourn me dead; think I am gone and wait for thee, for we shall meet again.

Romance in Relationships

Romance is a description we give to adventures of the heart—to relationships with special meaning in our lives.

Poets, lyricists, storytellers who focus on romantic love do a tender service for people who feel deeply but do better with child care, car repair, computers, and stocks and bonds than with the written word. Back in the forties Bob Eberly, a singer with Jimmy Dorsey's band, made famous a romantic song by Paul Madeira Mertz. During this era the rumblings of war stimulated people to be more thoughtful about their relationships. Values changed. In the face of war, love became precious.

Critics said that the song was ahead of its day, and indeed the words are applicable in our day, when the stress of life on the speedway gnaws away at time for sentiment. Read these words. Remember . . . yearn . . . dream . . . think of good ways of showing appreciation to the one who is important to you. Never underestimate the power of romance.

In this world of ordinary people
Extr'ordinary people

I'm glad there is you—
In this world of over-rated pleasures
Of under-rated treasures
I'm glad there is you.
I'll live to love, I'll love to live
With you beside me.
This role so new
I'll muddle thru'
With you to guide me.
In this world
Where many, many play at love
And hardly any stay in love,
I'm glad there is you,
More than ever,
I'm glad there is you.

44

Love's Afterglow

A distinguished judge knew that his earthly days were numbered. He had loved his wife dearly for more than sixty years. And though she was much younger than he, she had loved him long before he'd noticed the little teenager who hung around while he visited with her older brother. Now, with the end in sight, he worried about leaving her, and he worried about her funeral that surely would come one day! He wanted people to really know about her. He wanted justice done in her behalf. He knew that most of what he had done in life was largely due to her influence, her skill in bringing him around to the right social behavior and mellow, merciful attitude.

He called a good neighbor over late one evening, indicating that he wanted to say good-bye as well as to ask a few favors.

"In return, I'll take your greetings to anyone you love in heaven —if I can find them," he said, laughing a little.

What he wanted was for a neighborly interest to be taken in his beloved "partner in life," as he called her in reverence. Easy, pleasant assignment. Accepted.

Next he handed over a copy of a poem, written by an unknown author, which the judge had dedicated to his wife; he wanted to be certain that it was read at her funeral. This request sounded easy enough to carry out, but after those two special people had passed on, their mature children were of another mind. They wanted no such sentimentality at their mother's funeral. "When you are dead, you are dead. Funerals are for the living," one son explained to the woman who had made the promise to the judge.

This poem was not read at that wonderful wife's funeral. But maybe you have someone you love that it will suit just as well.

> Sometimes when day draws to its close
> The departing sun will throw
> Back to the world in fond farewell
> A lovely afterglow.
> I wish that I might so live
> That when my sun of life sinks low
> I might reflect to those I love
> A lovely afterglow.

45

To Mother with Love

Mother's love is one of the nearest things to Christlike love, because it typifies ultimate concern and caring. In return for their love mothers finally win a satisfying outpouring of love and gratitude.

At a tender memorial service for the mother of six sons and one daughter a fitting tribute was paid, with one son, Kevin W. Anderson, as spokesperson.

What is reprinted here was prepared especially for Virginia W. Anderson, a beloved teacher. Because it represents many people's feelings about their mothers, it is included here.

> I stand to pay a final family tribute to our mother, who was both an angel and an artist.
>
> Abraham Lincoln once wrote: "All that I am or ever hope to be I owe to my angel mother." Those words capture precisely how I feel about my mother—how all of her children feel about her. All that we are or ever hope to be we owe to her. In our family we believe in angels because we have lived with one.
>
> Mother was also an artist with an extraordinary gift. The story is told that Michelangelo was once asked how he created from marble such masterpieces as *David, Moses,* and the *Pietà*. He responded that he did not create them. He simply saw them imprisoned in stone and set about to set them free.
>
> Mother was the Michelangelo of the soul. She had the gift to see beyond a person's rough-hewn exterior to the beauty and potential captive within. She spent her life gently chiseling, shaping, and polishing to set us free.
>
> She was an artist whose paints were her personality and

virtue, whose canvas was her family, friends, and students. She painted happiness and joy into the life of everyone she met. Although we are now separated for a season, the memory of Mother will not be forgotten. How can it be? Her art is too well manifest in the lives of those she loved. For as I look out over this gathering, I see a gallery of Mother's masterpieces. In your faces I see her bold brushwork and the beauty and flourish of her paints: love and charity, faith and hope, dignity and courage. That is Mother's living legacy and our rich inheritance.

Although today we bury the body that Mother once wore, we do not bury Mother. She is an angel still, and now she works her art in heavenly realms.

In final tribute, I simply say, the greatest pride I have is this: that I am my mother's son.

When Love Is Done

The poet Francis William Bourdillon wrote:

> The night has a thousand eyes,
>   And the day but one;
> Yet the light of the bright world dies
>   With the dying sun.
>
> The mind has a thousand eyes,
>   And the heart but one;
> Yet the light of a whole life dies
>   When love is done.

I remember interviewing Sister Elva Cowley, wife of Elder Matthew Cowley, for a magazine article on grief. She courageously shared her feelings about the trauma of losing one's constant companion and about the way comfort comes. She was not a new widow, she was a wise one. It hadn't been all that long since her beloved husband died in his sleep in a motel across the street from the site of the Los Angeles Temple, where they had recently attended cornerstone laying ceremonies.

Then weeks passed when the sun didn't shine for her. Clear skies, blue and bright, presented only grey days. People passed on the street or talked in lobbies, their faces wreathed in the happiness of relationship. She wondered how they could smile! What was there to smile about in such a dark world? She was filled with self-pity, loneliness, aching longing for precious companionship. Faith in eternal life and ultimate togetherness was one thing; living without one's love was something else again.

She finally took work and diversion by acting as a receptionist at the Primary Children's Hospital. The tragedies of innocent children and worried parents were a daily parade. Then one day the most pathetic case of malformation in an infant was brought to her desk. Sister Cowley's own grief seemed nothing to bear in the face of such a pitiful situation, such a demanding caring of one human for another. One-sided love, it seemed to her. Sister Cowley questioned the mother about how she could stand such a tragedy.

"I know I am blessed," chirped the mother. "I know I am loved by God. I feel it within me every time I care for this baby. God sent it to me because he knew I would love it enough—I wanted a baby so badly."

Sister Cowley's prayers changed from personal need to endless thanks for what God had given her in relationship and certainty.

With a hand in God's, love is, after all, never done.

47

Good-bye, Love...

Love isn't necessarily over, though a relationship may be. Love is a thing of the heart and mind. Proximity isn't all there is to loving. You'll see, if you don't already know.

There are so many kinds of loving and so many ways to be separated: a bishopric is dissolved; a marriage is ended by death or demand; friends are pulled apart by war, work, transfer, or the Ten Commandments.

Every separation has a little of death in it. How else would we learn to endure the now and to hope for eternity? But the heart of that relationship is still in you. And the memories of it all mark your mind.

So when you have known love and then endured separation, know that the heart is only bruised but not broken. A broken heart is cumbersome baggage. Keep your margins straight and your ideals polished. Chalk up some good deeds. Discipline yourself to give and to love by duty or by rote. Thank God for love and loving and learning. Move forward among others to spread drops of honey where there were none before.

48

Ah! Offspring!

Mothers are known for their ultimate concern for their children. Fathers are famous for their quiet pride and fierce loyalty for the namesakes they don't quite understand.

But there is a time when the welling up of love in the heart is almost overwhelming. It is when mother and father see their children perform in excellence, achieve in accordance with their abilities, and, above all, walk in righteousness. At such times there is no tribute grand enough to pay the blessed crop of the next generation who call your house "home" and the people therein "my family"!

In the Third Epistle of John, verse 4, it is written this way: "I have no greater joy than to hear that my children walk in truth." And more, "And this is love, that we walk after his commandments" (2 John 1:6).

Grandpa Is My Friend

A friend is someone who loves you anyway . . . and always.

When something wonderful happens you want to share it with someone like that—a friend. This letter from a ten-year-old says it well:

Dear Grandpa:

I went fishing with my dad and a friend and his son. On the 31st throughout the 1st. We were at Nia Bay, it's the Farwest Resort. We caught 8 silver salmon. And I caught the biggest one, 10 or 11 pounds.

Love you!

Benson

Love Thy Stepchildren

The weeping woman would not be comforted. She was emotionally choked with self-reproach because she didn't love her stepchildren. She was choked with recrimination for her own inability to weld this his-and-hers family into something pleasing before God. She was choked with near hate for her husband because he was taking sides with his children against her. She was without hope. There seemed no way out. She was frustrated because things had dragged on and on in extreme unpleasantness even though she had tried and tried to have it otherwise.

What did people do about a distressing home life if they didn't believe in divorce? What did they do about financial arrangements? What effect would all of this negativism have on the children? Was there a solution anywhere? How could she have been so wrong in such an important decision? She had prayed about it. . . .

She had come for counsel. The counsel she received included these several points:

1. With God nothing is impossible, even loving your stepchildren. God gives no commandment unless he opens a way for us to keep it. Loving others as ourselves—even loving our enemies—is the great commandment. Remember, nothing is impossible with God's help.

2. Remember that children—even stepchildren so totally different from your own—are of great worth to God. Treat them as such. Begin by treating them as you would members of a Sunday School or Primary class. Then treat them as little friends. Treat them as precious to someone you love—their father.

3. Stop expecting total satisfaction in love to be part of your relationship with your stepchildren. Count your blessings. Build them up—poor innocents! Deliberately plan ways to delight them and serve them. Put others before self, right? You'll see it works.

4. Believe in the power of God to renew love, to endow with love, to heighten spiritual gifts promised in the case of faithfulness. Keep God's commandments (to love thy neighbor—thy stepchildren!—as thyself). He said, "This is my commandment, That ye love one another, as I have loved you" (John 15:12). He didn't suggest, he commanded. He didn't say to do the best you can, he said to love with a superior love, as he loves us *all*—darling or not!

Loving and the increased ability to love, unfeigned, come from God, who *is* love. Faith precedes the miracle of love, too. Believe, apply, reap the blessings.

And the woman was comforted.

Love among Fathers and Daughters

Teresa was in love.

So was her fiancé.

They wanted to be married as soon as possible, but for them love came once to a customer and it was worth doing right.

"Right" meant being married in the temple, surrounded by special loved ones from among family and friends. Teresa's father was truly a "special loved one" to her. All the days of her life she and her dad had been close. They'd had good times, great talks. Their loyal efforts on behalf of each other never failed. They provided protection and support. They exchanged laughter and tears on appropriate occasions.

Teresa would never forget the tears that filled Dad's eyes when she lost the school election. Now that is a friend—and a friend like that is a loved one! A loved one is someone who can't change what makes you hurt but who will cry with you. If it is your father, all the better.

There were two things Teresa wanted for her wedding—she wanted to be married in the temple and she wanted her dad there. The first was possible, but the second—well, Teresa's father didn't qualify for a recommend to go into the temple.

So Teresa waited and waited and waited. She didn't scold, complain, or criticize. She explained! And she went on loving her father, anyway.

Two years passed before the waiting was over. Teresa's love melted her father into personal preparation appropriate for obtaining the temple experience. And the day came.

When the ceremony was over Teresa went straight into her father's arms. She closed her eyes, and all the sweetness of life at home with a loving friend for a father passed before her eyes in a flash. She whispered in his ear, "Oh, Daddy! Daddy! My first and always sweetheart!"

It was a moment to remember. It was a lesson to learn. This father—this first sweetheart—was no threat to the new husband. Whoever Teresa loved, her father loved as well.

Father Anderson had a gift for loving. He looked upon people with delight and approval. He was generous in his enjoyment of their abilities and accomplishments. He was particularly proud of his new daughter-in-law when she performed a tender reading at the Christmas program in church. He asked that she would recite it again at the family Christmas party.

She did. He wept and loved it. And a tradition was born. Each year, when the children had presented their version of the sacred Christmas pageant and had finished their little talent show, and just before Grandma read Luke 2 from the Bible, Father Anderson would turn to his daughter-in-law and with a face wreathed in love and his misty eyes twinkling, he would politely ask if she would recite "David Star of Bethlehem."

The time came when Father Anderson passed away. And then, too soon—out of timing really—the daughter-in-law passed on, as well. The family felt sure that Father Anderson would be there to greet her on the other side of the veil, and that in honor of that great occasion he would smile and twinkle and invite her to give his favorite reading for the heavenly hosts.

Then there is the incident of the father who, for his daughter, drops his own life for the moment in order to crisis-shop the hosiery section of a department store.

The facts:

The father (Mike) is a young doctor and a member of a stake presidency—a very busy man. But he looks at his Emily and thinks, *Love you!*

The mother is away at an important meeting. She left her daughter looking great in a new dress with new black designer panty hose to complete the outfit.

The daughter is hysterical. Mother's gone. Dad's home, but well —what does he know about such things as snagging and running the panty hose just minutes before the date is due at the door!

Emily is right. Dad doesn't really know about such things, but he can try in the name of love.

He races to the store and is baffled by the wide selection —*Black, yes! But what size, type? Queen—she's a queen to me. Support? She has mine. Tummy control? Good grief, what will women think of next!* Finally he just buys one of each. Better safe than a ruined evening.

Love among fathers (or fathers-in-law) and daughters can have its own rewards. And having a loving father can steer a girl toward finding Heavenly Father loveable, too.

52

Love among Wise Men

In April 1842, about a month and a half after the organization of the Relief Society, Joseph Smith told the women of that society: "Let this Society teach women how to behave towards their husbands, to treat them with mildness and affection. When a man is borne down with trouble, when he is perplexed with care and difficulty, if he can meet a smile instead of an argument or a murmur—if he can meet with mildness, it will calm down his soul and soothe his feelings; when the mind is going to despair, it needs a solace of affection and kindness. . . .

". . . Never give a cross or unkind word to your husbands, but let kindness, charity and love crown your works henceforward."[17]

Brigham Young spoke in the Bowery in Salt Lake City on June 15, 1856, and gave some counsel which should motivate couples to pause and consider their situation: "When the wife secures to herself a glorious resurrection, she is worthy of the full measure of the love of the faithful husband, but never before. And when a man has passed through the veil, and secured to himself an eternal exaltation, he is then worthy of the love of his wife and children."[18]

George A. Smith was a member of the Quorum of the Twelve Apostles during the early years of the restored Church. He was greatly loved for his helpfulness and his benevolence. He figured prominently in the affairs of the Church and community in southern Utah, and St. George, Utah, was reputedly named after him. He was a cousin of the Prophet Joseph Smith and was keenly interested in the happenings of those early days. He came west with the Saints, was involved in many important events that transpired, and kept careful record of these events.

For example, on one occasion he explained how the Saints were governed by prophets and why the system worked. How, he asked, could Joseph Smith get so many men to leave their homes and travel the world and build up the kingdom? Many of the people he personally never saw. How did Brigham Young successfully control the rapidly growing number of Latter-day Saints? Elder Smith answered:

> It is by the power of that magic which wins hearts; by the power of those external principles of salvation which exist in God and in his faithful servants. Every man knows that in Brigham Young he has a friend and a father, and that when he counsels, instructs, corrects, or reproves, it is with the spirit of a father to his children—he corrects them for their own good; hence every person fears to do wrong and desires to do right, and, so far as this principle extends, Israel is governed by love and charity, by that strong bond of eternal truth which will make peace throughout the earth.[19]

This same George A. Smith was the grandfather of President George Albert Smith, who carried on his grandfather's tradition of an exemplary, loving demeanor toward his fellowmen. President Smith, eighth President of the Church, is buried in the Salt Lake City Cemetery near an impressively shaped marker inscribed with these words: "I believe in the brotherhood of man; we are all God's children; I love everyone."

President David O. McKay usually wore a white suit. He was tall, with a well-formed, masculine build. His white hair was wavy and abundant. What a handsome man! Women were seen to weep when he came onto the pulpit area of the Salt Lake Tabernacle or walked unannounced down the aisle of their neighborhood chapel (something he rather liked doing!).

On one occasion the "old folks" day was under way at Liberty Park in Salt Lake City, Utah. My husband was a young bishop then, and so we were obliged to participate. We took our four little children. It was exciting when President McKay surprised us all with a personal visit. Women wept and the old men had misty eyes, too!

We took our children close to President McKay so that they could see a prophet. He looked at these little children of ours for a moment, waving his hand in greeting. Then he suddenly said, "Oh, come here and let me have a hug!" And they did. Each one was lifted and encircled in his arms.

President and Sister McKay liked to escape to the theater when they could. One night there was a special movie shown in downtown Salt Lake, and we happened to find a parking place in front of the theater. As the program finished we got in our car, and when we realized that we were parked next to the McKays, we stayed to watch. They were unaware of us.

He guided her by the elbow to the passenger side of the car—the side next to our car. He opened the door to help her in and she turned to him, smiled her wonderful smile, and said graciously, "Thank you, Dade!" ("Dade" was her special name for him.)

It was a lasting example to my husband and me—how men and women should treat each other even when they don't think they're being watched.

It was June conference about 1939. A large group of selected young people from Salt Lake Valley made a visit to the home of President Heber J. Grant to give him a scroll expressing their commitment to keep the Word of Wisdom. I was one of those youths.

We gathered on the lush lawn of his avenue home, which overlooked Capitol Hill across City Creek Canyon and the valley below. It was impressive to us.

President Grant had a trim goatee and wore suspenders over a crisp shirt with the cuffs turned back. He greeted us warmly, then stood attentively while the scroll was read and presented. He spoke a few words of encouragement and of witness about the Word of Wisdom and about keeping promises, such as we had just made with him. I have not forgotten the sudden, sweeping, sacred and sweet warm feeling that came over me—over most of us, according to the conversation on the way home—when he finished his talk with us.

"I love you! Don't forget, I love you!"

Following a major address at Brigham Young University in Provo, Utah, President Spencer W. Kimball leaned toward his wife, Camilla, and gave her a quick kiss on the cheek—much to the delight of thousands of students, faculty, and guests in the congregation. I happened to visit with him two days later and mentioned the pleasure it gave me to see that public show of affection toward his wife.

He had the gift of a quick wit, and he retorted, "And it wasn't that bad, either!"

And then with more soberness, he added, "Tell the sisters to kiss their husbands more. They don't get enough loving."

It was the dedication of the New York World's Fair in May 1964. The executives of the fair had been reluctant to allow the Mormons to have a pavilion. But it was accomplished—an impressive effort. Officials of the fair and most of the General Authorities and their special guests were gathered for a ceremony of dedication, an idea which was surprising and new to the New Yorkers.

As the program progressed, the Spirit of the Lord increased. The final thrill was a rousing number by the choir of the Manhattan Ward in New York City. Melva Niles and Robert Peterson, Broadway stars, were among those participating. The choir sang "The Spirit of God Like a Fire," with Melva rendering an obbligato that brought a sudden rush of tears to our eyes.

President Joseph Fielding Smith was usually quite staid at the pulpit, seldom exhibiting emotion. But he, too, was overcome with the power of the Spirit in those moments. He was on the front row of the temporary stage. His wife, Jessie Evans Smith, sat on the first row of chairs set up for the audience. As he sniffled and teared up, she reached across that narrow space to offer him her handkerchief. It was trimmed with wide lace and was distinctly feminine looking.

He resisted. She insisted. He resisted.

The musical number reached its highest peak. The Spirit was overwhelming and President Smith was in some tender trouble. Finally, Sister Smith got up from her chair and put the handkerchief in his hand and sat down. He used it, too!

This remains one of my favorite memories of husband/wife interaction.

President Harold B. Lee was dressed in white to conduct a ceremony of marriage in the Salt Lake Temple. The usual procedure is for the officiating authority first to talk with the couple about love and marriage, loyalty, commitment, tenderness, and other appropriate things. He then performs the holy sealing ceremony that binds the man and woman together for time and all eternity.

This particular time in June 1972 President Lee immediately performed the ceremony. Then he talked.

It was a startling departure. The only time I've seen this done.

He explained that love is a gift. Certain helpful instructions about increasing their love as they lived together in patience, consideration, refinement, and sacrifice were important, but this part of the talk was not as important as the sealing ceremony and its promises.

He explained the switch, "Rather than have you distracted by temporal counsel, I wanted you to be conscious of what was going on here—eternal covenants and promises you participated in.''

President Ezra Taft Benson and Sister Flora Benson took us on a memorable drive through their beloved country on the Utah-Idaho border. We saw their childhood haunts and listened to their precious recollections. Then we visited the cemetery where the family burial plot is.

There is a sheltered corner with an oversized granite marker bearing President and Sister Benson's names and the names of all their children. At the time of this writing all of them are still alive, but they are ready to be together in death and beyond, just as they are in this life.

President David O. McKay and President Hugh B. Brown had been together in a First Presidency meeting for several hours during the morning on one particular day.

At this time President and Sister McKay were living in a special suite in the Hotel Utah. Following lunch President McKay started his walk from the hotel to his office in Church headquarters up the street.

President Brown was walking from headquarters toward the hotel and they met. People on the street knew who these great leaders were, but they were startled to see them stop, greet each other in joy, embrace warmly and visit in laughter—an obviously affectionate exchange—and then move in opposite directions to their appointed destinations.

Only an hour or two had passed since they were together, and yet their love and devotion was such that they embraced when they met.

How far most of us have yet to go!

Love among the Ancients

It is fascinating to read the scriptures just for the story line, for the joy of understanding relationships. Love among the prophets reminds us that God should be in *our* relationships, in *our* loving, as well.

What kinds of affectionate tributes do we find in the scriptures?

The devotion of David and Jonathan is legend. They could have been natural rivals, yet they loved each other and together made covenants of loyalty and friendship before the Lord. Jonathan, you remember, was King Saul's son. David was married to Michal, Jonathan's sister. He, not Jonathan, was marked to be king after Saul.

Consider the elements in their exchange of love which brought about life-saving loyalty:

Jonathan said to David in a covenant before the Lord, "The Lord be between me and thee, and between my seed and thy seed for ever" (1 Samuel 20:42).

And Saul said unto David, who spared Saul's life, "Thou art more righteous than I: for thou hast rewarded me good, whereas I have rewarded thee evil" (1 Samuel 24:17).

When Jonathan and Saul were killed in battle, David and his men grieved mightily. David's famous lament includes these stirring lines, "Saul and Jonathan were lovely and pleasant in their lives, and in their death they were not divided: they were swifter than eagles, they were stronger than lions" (2 Samuel 1:23).

Joseph was taken down into Egypt after having been sold by his brothers in a jealous rage. He became loved by Pharaoh for his good works, his loyalty, his integrity. Joseph prophesied to Pharaoh about the seven years of famine and suggested that food be stored against the day. "And Pharaoh said unto his servants, Can we find such a one as this is, a man in whom the Spirit of God is? And Pharaoh said unto Joseph, . . . there is none so discreet and wise as thou art." (Genesis 41:38–39.)

With all the trouble among God's children recorded in the Old Testament and with all the trouble known to us in our own time, still the eloquence of love—of regard and respect—shared among Heavenly Father's children on earth can save the day!

In the Book of Mormon there is an account that rouses one's blood—the account of people with affection for each other meeting after a season of separation. Alma was journeying from the land of Gideon to the land of Manti, and to his absolute astonishment he met with the sons of Mosiah, who were traveling toward the land of Zarahemla. He loved them. They had been with him at the time the angel first appeared unto him. They'd shared sacred experiences—an occurrence which always heightens people's regard for each other.

"Alma did rejoice exceedingly to see his brethren; and what added more to his joy, they were still his brethren in the Lord; yea, and they had waxed strong in the knowledge of the truth; for they were men of a sound understanding and they had searched the scriptures diligently, that they might know the word of God. But this is not all; they had given themselves to much prayer, and fasting; therefore they had the spirit of prophecy, and the spirit of revelation, and when they taught, they taught with power and authority of God." (Alma 17:2–3.)

With qualifications like that, of course they were loved!

Studying King Benjamin's final counsel to his subjects, in terms of love and devoted relationships, provides specific guidance today for our own behavior toward each other. If we are wise we will try to become more like Jesus.

King Benjamin says, "As ye have come to the knowledge of the glory of God, or if ye have known of his goodness and have tasted of his love, and have received a remission of your sins, which causeth such exceedingly great joy in your souls, even so I would that ye should remember, and always retain in remembrance, the greatness of God, . . . his goodness and long-suffering towards you'' (Mosiah 4:11).

Then the good king tells the people (and us, too) to humble themselves, to stand steadfast in the faith, and thus they will always be filled with the love of God; they will not have a mind to injure one another, but to live peaceably, to render to every man what he needs; and they will teach their children not to quarrel but to love and to serve one another (see Mosiah 4:11–15).

Statement of the First Presidency

The following statement, ''God's Love for All Mankind,'' was prepared by the First Presidency of The Church of Jesus Christ of Latter-day Saints and issued February 15, 1978. The content reminds us of the blessing and duty to love God and all mankind.

Based upon ancient and modern revelation, The Church of Jesus Christ of Latter-day Saints gladly teaches and declares the Christian doctrine that all men and women are brothers and sisters, not only by blood relationship from common mortal progenitors, but also as literal spirit children of an Eternal Father.

The great religious leaders of the world such as Mohammed, Confucius, and the Reformers, as well as philosophers including Socrates, Plato, and others, received a portion of God's light. Moral truths were given to them by God to enlighten whole nations and to bring a higher level of understanding to individuals.

The Hebrew prophets prepared the way for the coming of Jesus Christ, the promised Messiah, who should provide salvation for all mankind who believe in the gospel.

Consistent with these truths, we believe that God has given and will give to all peoples sufficient knowledge to help them on their way to eternal salvation, either in this life or in the life to come.

We also declare that the gospel of Jesus Christ, restored to his Church in our day, provides the only way to a mortal life of happiness and a fulness of joy forever. For those who have not received this gospel, the opportunity will come to them in the life hereafter if not in this life.

Our message therefore is one of special love and concern for the eternal welfare of all men and women, regardless of religious belief, race, or nationality, knowing that we are truly brothers and sisters because we are the sons and daughters of the same Eternal Father.[20]

It is not surprising that a Christian church should take such a stand, but for the Church of Jesus Christ to issue this statement as an official stand to be followed is impressive. It broadens our understanding and should prod our resolve to respect all human life; to be a friend to others after the manner of a true disciple of Christ; to love God and all mankind.

Love in Return

Oh, to read again the exquisite words of the vision of Nephi and to discover through prayer God's love for us! There is wisdom and even joy in making a study of God's words about love—his for us and ours, in return, for him.

The following uplifting lines from the writings of Nephi are important clues about the exchange of love between God and man: "And the angel said unto me: Behold the Lamb of God, yea, even the Son of the Eternal Father! Knowest thou the meaning of the tree which thy father saw? And I answered him, saying: Yea, it is the love of God, which sheddeth itself abroad in the hearts of the children of men; wherefore, it is the most desirable above all things. And he spake unto me, saying: Yea, and the most joyous to the soul." (1 Nephi 11:21–23.)

The love of God flows into the hearts of men.

The love of God is most desirable above all things.

The love of God is the most joyous to the soul.

Here is a personal experience told by Maureen Derrick Keeler that proves the point:

As a young single woman in my late twenties, I had been reviewing the direction of my life and considering some major changes. An unwelcome birthday had left me feeling older than I wanted to be; and, like many single members of the Church, I felt I had failed to reach some important personal goals. It seemed that I needed some specific direction from the Lord. So, for the first time in my life, I asked my priesthood leader to give me a blessing. This good man prepared himself by fasting, and suggested that I do the same. We met early one radiant Sunday morning.

As he spoke the words of the blessing, I listened intently for answers and solutions. But in that I was disappointed; the Lord had wisely left me to find my own way. Instead, he blessed me with what I *really* needed: an undeniable personal witness of his love for me. The blessing spoke of God's specific awareness of my life and my problems. As examples of his constant influence were called to my mind, the Spirit confirmed the truthfulness of each. My heart overflowed with love and gratitude, springing from some untouched place deep within me. For the first time I had really experienced God's love, and I could respond to him not only with my loyalty, but with my own love in return.

I have often pondered the effects of that experience. How could a knowledge of God's love for me endow my life with such permanent strength? To me, the wonder of it was that God was so near, that he was completely aware of my most secret sorrows and fears—even my troubled midnight thoughts. I was not alone! His was a love that enabled me to "let go," and to realize that even though my goals had not been achieved exactly as I felt they should be, God's plan, whatever it was, would be better than my own.[21]

We turn to God with our hearts full of gratitude for his blessings and with hope, at the very least, that he will hear our prayers. As we yield our hearts to him, as did the prodigal son to his earthly father, he rushes forth to greet us and we feel his love and love him in return. And it makes all the difference.

Love as Commanded

The obedient easily witness that keeping God's commandments brings forth the promised blessings. The Lord has said that if we would keep his commandments we should abide in love. And he commanded that we should love each other: "These things have I spoken unto you, that my joy might remain in you, and that your joy might be full. This is my commandment, That ye love one another, as I have loved you." (John 15:11–12.)

The promises, the blessings hinging upon that commandment, seem enormously wonderful. We will have his "joy" to "remain" in us! He laid down his life for us, but what we have to do is give others a chance by sending forth the comfortable "vibes" of love!

The Apostle John, in chapter 4 of his first epistle, had some beautiful things to say about love:

"God is love." (v. 8)

"If we love one another, God dwelleth in us, and his love is perfected in us." (v. 12)

"He that dwelleth in love dwelleth in God, and God in him." (v. 16)

"He that loveth not his brother whom he hath seen, how can he love God whom he hath not seen?" (v. 20)

"And this commandment have we from him, That he who loveth God love his brother also." (v. 21)

We learn by definition. Commandments are "intended to control our thoughts and desires as well as our acts."[22]

A command is a directive given by one in authority, and *obedience* on the part of the person addressed is *expected*.

As we keep the great commandment to love God and all men, life will be sweeter and more peaceful on earth, and after death reunions will be not only expected but anticipated.

Two things to remember:

1. We do err unless we admit that only by keeping this particular commandment to love can we exist together in God's presence as a close family circle, having eternal increase after the manner of God. Delaying the day of our repentance, of our appropriate behavior in spirit and letter, proves us foolish.

2. Loving one another surely must apply to our feelings toward spouse, neighbor, mother-in-law, stepchildren, our son's wife, our husband's first wife, and the "clients" of the census taker—children of God, too.

Abide in Love

God expects us to abide in love. He wants us to experience the change of heart—the mellowing, the yielding, the humbling, the obedience—that allows his Spirit to enter our lives and influence our behavior. Then we can abide in love. (See John 15:10.)

Countless people have testified about the wonder that fills their hearts and minds and the joy that fills their lives as they conscientiously try to love all people. A change actually occurs in them. A miracle happens.

I heard President Harold B. Lee share a remarkable experience —an awakening—that occurred in his life during the period following the death of President Joseph Fielding Smith, when President Lee knew he was to be the new President of the Church. President

Lee humbled himself before God. It was a time of close communion —an outpouring of gratitude, seeking comfort from anxiety, and praying for direction to help people. Then a wonderful vision crossed his mind. There was a sweeping, flowing parade of people of all colors, situations, ages, and place. He knew that they were all the people of the earth for whom he would have special concern— whether they knew it or not! The miracle was that as they passed he was flooded with a love for them that increased as more passed by, until he was overwhelmed. His heart was about to burst with love and joyful responsibility. He knew he would have God's help, for President Lee knew that not only he himself loved these people but also Heavenly Father loved them all, equally.

A young missionary had just arrived in the South American field of his assigned labor. He boarded a bus in a small town and stood at the front, for a moment, looking for a seat. He was in a state of culture shock. For the first time in his nineteen years he was in the minority in terms of skin color, clothing, amenities. He sat down and put his head in his hands. He was the only white person on the bus. He felt bereft and frightened. He wanted to flee—to find his way home in the quickest possible way. He wondered what he was doing there.

Then he remembered the incredible night at home just a few months before, when he had prayed on his knees for a witness that Jesus lived and wanted him to go on a mission. And wonder of wonders, it came! He was personally filled with that warm, abiding assurance that he was to serve a mission and that the Lord was mindful of *him.*

Remembrance of that experience gave him courage now. He uttered a brief, silent prayer and then lifted his head from his hands. He turned to the lady beside him on the bus and smiled. She smiled back, then leaned across the aisle to say something to her neighbor in their native language. The neighbor smiled at the missionary. The contagion of that welcome spread around the bus.

Suddenly the missionary's heart turned over with affection for these new friends. He knew he'd come to the right place to serve. Two years later, during his homecoming report, he wept as he spoke of them.

58

Love All People

God loves all people. He expects us to do the same. Our goal is to try to become more like him. We begin by keeping his commandments, gradually improving our ability to do so. We start with a single act and move forward as a way of life.

Suddenly there is no more contention in the land—the heart, the home, the neighborhood, the city, the nation, the world.

Is there precedent for this?

Yes. The city of Enoch was so committed to Christ that the whole city was finally taken into heaven!

Yes, again. In the Book of Mormon we learn that for two hundred years after the Savior had taught and blessed the people on the American continent there was no contention in the land because the love of God was in their hearts: "There were no envyings, nor strifes, nor tumults, nor whoredoms, nor lyings, nor murders, nor any manner of lasciviousness; and surely there could not be a happier people among all the people who had been created by the hand of God. . . . And how blessed were they! For the Lord did bless them in all their doings." (4 Nephi 1:16, 18.)

Among the blessings they enjoyed was the healing of the sick. In the name of Jesus Christ the disciples healed the sick, raised the dead, and caused the lame to walk and the blind to see.

People may not be perfect, and surely none go through life without trials, but it is attitude and behavior, the ways of coping and helping, that make the difference. When people esteem others as themselves they are quick to reach and lift and praise and rejoice in another's success and weep over another's heartbreak. When the heart isn't locked up in self-centeredness it is open to God's influence and sweetening spirit. It is then that war—caused by anger, contention, jealousy, and greed—is crowded out. On every level there is peace.

The outcome of this attitude is families who not only exchange hugs, loving-kindness, and patience, but also never give up on each other. From family to friends and neighbors ripples the ever-widening circle of good influence.

For abiding in love, first try to apply gospel principles, get over the problems, straighten the ways, and love each other as God's children. No matter what the minute configurations are, we all are part of the grand family of God!

And the family of God abides in love.

Forgive Them!

Consider this incident in the light of love—God's love, personal love, family love, Judeo-Christian love. It is true. I was there.

In 1976 a government-funded women's conference was held, staged to the tune of five million dollars, for the purpose of promoting equal rights for women and approving certain resolutions to be forwarded to Congress for their consideration. Representative women were sent from each state in the Union as delegates.

During the final sessions a thing so shameful happened as to leave thoughtful, caring women sick at heart and frightened for the wholesome welfare of all Americans.

The organizers of the conference had blocked the general public from their balcony seats and reserved these sections for those who supported the idea of "sexual and affectional freedom." Women wearing badges proclaiming that they were lesbians filled the balconies. The convention floor below was, of course, filled with the conference delegates, the majority of whom represented stable, traditional values, who were home and family loving and God-fearing.

This particular Sunday afternoon the resolutions regarding "sexual and affectional freedom" and "abortion" were presented for the vote of the delegates.

Afterwards it was learned that this government-funded, tax-supported conference was stacked by the planners. For example, during the discussion period on the aforementioned sticky subjects, the chair's recognition of delegates lining up by floor microphones came only if the delegate wore a prearranged signal ribbon. The vote in favor of abortion carried.

There was such an uproar of approval from the balcony, from the committees in reserved seating for special guests on the convention floor, and from a portion of the delegates themselves that it was startling. And it was allowed to swell and grow and prolong. Doubled fists and upstretched arms were thrust upward as the chant "Choice" was picked up and passed on among this particular segment of the thousands of women in that Texas convention hall. Then from the back of the hall a small group of women protesting this action formed themselves into a body to march forward in front of the delegates. They sang a mournful funeral dirge version of "God Bless America." They carried full-colored posters of unborn babies. Their presentation wasn't as noisy or vehement as the other, but it got attention when they passed before the pro-abortion group, and one of the latter pushed her doubled fist into a poster and shredded it before all of our eyes. (The fetus, you see, was thus symbolically destroyed!)

It was sickening. Tears filled our eyes. We suddenly realized how misguided many women are, and we uttered a silent prayer, "God, forgive them, for they know not what they do." And we made a vow.

On the way home, I was sitting up front in the airplane and one of the delegates came past the others to kneel on the floor beside my seat. She said, "Sister Cannon, how bad do things have to get before Christ comes to save us?"

Still sick at heart, I paused before I answered her question. "It seems to me that it isn't how bad things have to get before Christ comes again. It must be how good do people have to be and how loving to form a nucleus to receive him!"

And we two, strangers at the beginning of the week, were going home to our different states, our somewhat different lives, but we lovingly hugged each other in recognition of shared values.

Love and Change

"The nearer we get to our heavenly Father, the more we are disposed to look with compassion on perishing souls," Joseph Smith said; "we feel that we want to take them upon our shoulders, and cast their sins behind our backs."[23]

The experience of Enos, as recorded in the Book of Mormon, is one of many examples proving that when we bask in the redeeming love of Christ, our thoughts turn to others. Enos describes how his soul hungered for forgiveness and for approval from the Lord. He went to a private place and cried out to God all day and night. Finally a voice said unto him the blessed words we all long to hear, "Thy sins are forgiven thee, and thou shalt be blessed" (Enos 1:5). Then Enos began to feel a desire for the welfare of his brethren. He poured out his whole soul unto God for them. Again the voice of the Lord came into his mind and promised him answer to *this* prayer; the Nephites would be blessed according to their righteousness. Enos's final prayer—this time for his brethren the Lamanites —was also answered; there would be salvation for them in some future day. And Enos rejoiced in his Savior.

The following lines were scribbled out among the notes taken during the Sunday morning session of April 1984 general conference. My soul had been lifted by one speaker who obviously had been abundantly blessed by the Holy Spirit.

Be Swift to Love

O Father, I have promised thee
    To humbly take His name,
To love thy children, do His will,
    And thus choice blessings claim.
Be swift, my soul, to love, to serve,
    To do His work today,
To meet the needs with fitting deeds
    Of lambs who've gone astray.
O Father, let me serve thy Son
    To move His kingdom forth,
To praise His name, and why He came;
    To help men know their worth.
Be swift, my soul, to heed Christ's call
    To love and feed His sheep.
I'll pray, be still, and learn His will
        And thus my promise keep.

61

Love and War

How love manifests itself in the lives of others is often inspiring and surprising.

During the latter part of the Vietnam War a conference for college-age youth was held at Asilomar Center on the coast of northern California. During the closing hours of the conference a testimony meeting was held. A young man just back from soldiering in Vietnam held the congregation in full attention as he related his experiences.

This young man loved the Lord and hated going to war, but he decided to put his trust in the Lord. He was rewarded with an outpouring of heavenly love and protection and blessings through terrible months.

He had decided he didn't want to kill anybody during this war. He carried a rifle but never had to fire it during eight months in Vietnam. On one occasion he managed to bring twenty-five of the "enemy" over to our side by talking them into it!

The drinking water was a treacherous situation in Vietnam most of the time. The soldier, a convert to the Church, was desperately thirsty. He prayed for help in finding pure water. Not long after, he and his group of military companions came upon a clear, cool stream in the jungle. It was a miracle to them!

He bore testimony that to him, finding the gospel in the midst of a wicked world was like finding a clear, cool stream in the midst of the dirty water.

He expressed love for the gospel and love for the Savior and witnessed to the changes that had happened in his life since he had been governed by Christlike love.

Love Is a Multiple

Love is a multiple—true enough. The longer you live, the more adventures you survive/enjoy in life; and the more you love, the more certain you are that if you love once you are more than likely to love again.

First-time parents insist that there never has been such a wonderful child as this first baby of theirs, nor will there be again. In fact the thoughts of a second child are almost frightening. The young parents are certain that the second, the third, and so on will suffer by comparison to the love that they feel for the first child.

Not so.

The miracle is that loving works. The second child (or second wife!), the third child, and more are loved as much as the first. The new President of the Church is loved and prayed for just as his predecessor was.

Friendship, loving relationships, romantic alliances have a time and a place for a certain fulfillment, but exclusive love for one person is a myth. We love each other in different ways and for different reasons, but love is a multiple. Love one, love another. Love once, love again. It becomes easier in the doing.

Listen again to Linda Ronstadt croon about the chance meeting of two parts of a former romance. "What's new? Pardon my asking what's new. Of course you couldn't know, I haven't changed, I still love you so!"

So the "Dear John" letter was written. Or a man meets and loves and marries a girl he met while away from home for medical school. But there is that girl he left behind . . .

Time passes. Life imposes change, and the two who vowed never to part marry for love, but not to each other. At the high school reunion twenty-five years later they meet again. Ah—everything has changed but nothing has changed. "What's new? . . . I still love you so!" And it's a gift. Love is a gift, not an opportunity to stir up mischief.

"O clasp we to our hearts for dear blessed dower; this close companioned inarticulate hour when twofold silence was the song of love," wrote Christina Rossetti. Fine, we say, but remembering is gratitude of the heart, not an open-door policy. Surely it is possible (and likely, if we're lucky) to find out that love is a multiple. How else could it be when God loves us all the same and we are to learn to be like him?

Love's Broad Reach

The broad reach of love includes what one person is willing to do for another person—and another, another, another! Hilde Goettig is such a person. Limited in activity because of her physical condition, nonetheless she finds ways to wrap people in love and lift their spirits.

There is a wonderful scripture that seems to have been written especially for Hilde Goettig.

In Colossians 2:2 we read of hearts "comforted, being knit together in love."

Knit is defined, in part, as "to join or grow together closely and firmly."[24] It can also mean "to weave, unite, link, join, tie, fasten, interlace, intertwine, bind."[25]

Having considered definitions, synonyms, let us consider the workings of love in this regard. Hilde is a skilled artisan with yarn, needles, and hooks—tools of knitting and crochet work. Over the years of her life, she has finished many lovely items of clothing and covering.

Her heart has been softened by illness and personal tragedy, and when someone she loves is stricken in a similar way, Hilde works literally around the clock to prepare a gorgeous afghan to bring comfort.

I have been blessed by her in this way, and am appreciative not only of the warmth the afghan provides but also of the example of Hilde and her warm, loving heart—her broad reach from her narrow place.

64

Love in the Fast Lane

We were in the fast lane trying to get the neighbor girl to school on time. The genial traffic cop on the corner flashed his flag in warning. We slowed down, and as we passed by him the young woman waved a warm hello and smiled at him.

We learned from her that "Uncle David," as the children called him, was loved by everybody. He was a kind of security blanket for the kindergartners. He was safety for fifth-grade girls running from boys with snowballs. He parted traffic for junior high students who tended to jaywalk because they were always late. To the seniors he stood as a reminder of the good side of the law—pleasantness and protection in the big world.

Besides this, he learned everyone's name and didn't forget a face as they grew up. And he smiled his good mornings. Uncle David was loved.

He knew it, too. The days the students got rides to school they waved at him out the window. And as our neighbor girl told us, her big sister waved at Uncle David all through her school days and right on past the birth of her second child!

Then Uncle David took sick and died, and many, many present and former school children walked past his coffin to soberly nod their thanks and farewells.

We learned something about love in the fast lane that day.

Love at Home

It's a wonder that so much love and affection abound in the world, it is such a difficult standard to live by. People are expected to love their enemies, folks who are of different races and religion and political belief! People are obliged to love their children when they are sassy, destructive, and personally messy. They are supposed to love old Grandma or Pa or Auntie Edith when they are senile, demanding, and personally messy.

The ideal of love and what people are actually able to generate in personal relationships under trying conditions are often marathons apart.

It is at home where the vital and joy-bringing celebrations take place. Ceremonies may be conducted in temples, mosques, cathedrals, chapels, and meetinghouses, but the observance must happen in families. It is there that individuals can be honored, sensitive interaction can occur, values can be cultivated and traditions cherished as importance is placed upon them and through usage.

Children are easier to love. They're new. But the harder test is how a family treats its old members. They are not only not new but also often incurable, helpless, cantankerous, and set in their ways, which aren't the ways of the current generation of family members!

Barbara Bush, wife of President George Bush, probably gained cultural immortality with her oft-quoted idea from the talk she gave to Wellesley graduates in June 1990. It is a winner! She suggested that children needed to be read to and hugged more, and that it wasn't so much what happened in the White House that was important, "it is what happens in *your* house!"

Yea!

Let there be love at home!

66

Funny about Love

Doris watched her husband slide his suit coat back off his arms and let it drop to the floor while he flexed his muscles and posed like Mr. American Anatomy. She wanted to drop through the floor, but she turned to her friend and whispered, "Why does Ken do this in a social gathering? Why *does* he do this? How can I love him?"

Doris and her husband were very young, very new at marriage, very insistent that each other be perfect in order to earn love's tenderness.

Her friend was older, wiser. "Did I ever tell you about my friend who complained for forty years because each night her husband dropped his dirty socks in a heap by the bedpost. When he died she cried—because the socks weren't there!"

"Come on, Martha. What am I to do?"

"Laugh with the rest of us."

"Laugh? I could die!"

"Look, Doris. You and Ken have a lot going for you. He could chase women! Don't die over this, honey. Button your lip and ignore it! Love Ken, anyway. Kiss him extra warmly tonight. Why make misery when you can make—"

"Love. Yeah, I know," murmured disbelieving Doris.

The years passed but not Ken's urge to show off his fantastic, fit condition—even though he was pushing seventy. Doris had learned to mask her feelings. One night at study group she and Martha sat together again while Ken performed the ritual fitness dance.

The two women looked at each other and laughed. Then Doris said something very significant to the study of love. She said, "Martha, I learned to endure this ridiculous show-off skit of Ken's. But now I look at him entertaining anyone who will watch and my heart turns over. He has been so good to me over the years that I have come to love him with a depth I never would have believed possible at the beginning. His muscle act *is* Ken. I love him *because* of it, now, not in spite of it.''

Funny about love. To give up on each other too soon is to lose the wonder of love.

Cleave with All Your Heart

We are familiar with such scriptural counsel as ''a man . . . shall cleave unto his wife,'' ''cleave to that which is good,'' ''cleave unto me with all your heart,'' ''cleave unto her and none else,'' ''light cleaveth unto light.''

To cleave means to join, to bring together, or to act together to form a continuous unit.

Covenants are made in marriage, the ultimate possibility of love. Promises are made to keep these covenants, and we should do our best to see that nothing happens that would short-circuit the power and promise of love. Living together in quiet desperation, hanging on with white knuckles, clenched fists, gritted teeth, and a joyless demeanor is not what keeping those covenants is all about. The gift of love rarely comes as the result of such ''efforts.''

Love is not a test of endurance, though everything possible should be worked out by both lovers so as not to mock God by willfully destroying this sacred gift of the Spirit.

Lovers aren't perfect people. This becomes clear when the ''love is blind'' stage passes. However, admiration for each other's efforts toward perfection and toward pleasing one another is part of the adventure. Perfection might prove boring to earthbound people!

Never forget to express love in the ways provided by God. Always cherish each other after the manner of the poets. The human soul is of great worth to God and also should be of great worth to lovers who have promised to cleave to each other and to God.

Constantly bring joy and riches into this intimate relationship. Strengthen the habit of a daily sharing of your love for each other, thus reminding yourselves of your personal commitments to each other: "I love you! I honor you! I am grateful to you for having me."

Remember, the ways of the world don't work—wickedness never was happiness. Look around and receive proof of that. The ways of God do work. Look around and receive proof of this truth. Cleave with all your heart and mark the increase in love.

Love's Forgiveness

A bishop lay in the throes of death. The shocking report from his doctor had given him six weeks to live. He was finally diagnosed as having a terminal brain tumor—the desperately fast-growing, painful variety.

The family determined and publicly announced to friends, Church members, and neighbors that they would prefer absolutely no personal visits. It was a kind of mandate that almost everyone honored.

Except two. These two pressured and coaxed their way into the presence of a man they loved and respected so much that they wanted to make peace with him. And it was allowed.

These two were women the bishop had excommunicated. He had handled the whole business with such understanding, support, and love that they wanted to have a proper reconciliation with him before he died. Not only for their sake but for his. They forgave him —even thanked him for loving them enough to let them learn the valuable lesson of repentance.

It has been said by Jean Paul Richter that "each departed friend is a magnet that attracts us to the next world."

Naturally!

Let's say it again. God is love. Love in us is a gift of God. We are children of a Heavenly Father whose capacity for love goes beyond our highest imaginings. But how we bask in that love!

There are those who have chosen to harden their hearts, whose choices and responses to circumstance (for whatever excuse or reason) have led them to conclude that love has escaped them —any kind of love. They insist they aren't the "loving" kind. Hmmm . . .

The December 25, 1948, issue of the *New York Times* had a thoughtful column about the joys of being home for the holidays, about the sweetness of family reunions, about following your bliss —home. There was one line especially worth remembering: "The joke is on those who maintain that it does not come natural to human beings to love one another."

Loving does come naturally to children of a loving God. If you have a problem with this idea, put it to the test. You'll see that it is true.

No Greater Love

It is recorded in John 15:13 that shortly before the crucifixion of the Lord Jesus Christ he said to his disciples: "Greater love hath no man than this, that a man lay down his life for his friends."

Not all of us are required to die for others. But we may want to shift our priorities in life to the point where we are willing to put aside our own desires and pursuits for the sake of someone we love.

Such was the experience of Allen E. Bergin. He wrote about how one evening, under the pressure of important professional work, he returned to the office. As he left he noticed his wife all alone in the kitchen, with no help from any of the older children, even, in the important and laborious task of processing and bottling grape juice for the family storage. He related:

As I drove toward my BYU office, I asked myself: "What great intellectual achievement will I make tonight that is more important than making grape juice? Even if I do write something fine, will my spending an extra evening on academic work be more important than what is happening at home?" The answer was obvious. I made a U-turn and drove back to the house. When I walked in, my wife said: "What happened? Did you run out of gas?" "No," I said. "I decided there wasn't anything down there more important than helping you make grape juice.''

As I rolled up my sleeves and put on an apron, I noticed tears in her eyes. We had a lovely, memorable evening together. Not only did we share work, we visited in depth and shared some tender moments. As our children arrived home, they were all affected by what was happening.[26]

Christ laid down his life—he chose to die for us, after taking upon himself the burdens of our mistakes and sins. This becomes more and more awe-inspiring to us as we grow in gospel understanding and inner spirituality. Would we be willing to do this for others? Loved ones, perhaps, but what about strangers?

It is a stunning experience to visit the Chapel of the Four Chaplains, an interfaith shrine in Philadelphia. To relive the sacrifice these four men made during World War II is to remember what loving others as ourselves is all about.

The four were George Lansing Fox, an ordained Methodist minister; Alexander David Goode, a Jewish rabbi; Clark Poling, a Yale Divinity School graduate; and John Washington, a Catholic priest. The four were assigned to the *Dorchester,* a ship that had been a luxury cruise liner before World War II. On February 3, 1943, the *Dorchester* took a mortal wound from a U-456. As it was sinking, chaos and panic reigned. The only hope came from the four chaplains, who suddenly appeared and calmly distributed life jackets, then guided the panic-stricken men over the side of the ship. The written account continues:

On the promenade deck, Second Engineer Grady Clark saw the chaplains coolly handing out life jackets from the locker until there were no more left. Then he watched in awe as they gave away their own.

By now the rail was awash, and Clark slipped into the frigid water. Looking back as he swam away, he saw the chaplains standing—their arms linked—braced against the slanting deck. They were praying.

Other men drew close. There were no more outcries, no panic, just words of prayer in Latin, Hebrew and English, addressed to the same God.

Then the stern came high out of the water, and the *Dorchester* slid down into the sea.

It should be remembered that the chaplains gave their jackets to whatever men came along—they didn't ask the men's religion so the Jew could give to the Jew and the Catholic to the Catholic.

One witness said, "It was the finest thing I have ever seen, or hope to see, this side of heaven."[27]

71

Love and Countenances

In about 83 B.C. Alma, the high priest according to the holy order of God, traveled about and preached a powerful sermon to the people in their cities and villages. He spoke of the ways in which salvation may be obtained. He told how the bonds of hell which had encircled their fathers became loosed through the love of Christ—how their souls had expanded and they had sung redeeming love.

Alma said to the people, "Have ye spiritually been born of God? Have ye received his image in your countenances? Have ye experienced this mighty change in your hearts? . . . If ye have felt to sing the song of redeeming love, I would ask, can ye feel so now?" (Alma 5:14, 26.)

When people truly know God they love him. When they love him they want to keep his commandments and do the works of righteousness. And they do sing of redeeming love!

May it be so with us.

Some people are born with a gift to make a point remain with us by using humor. In a certain Relief Society class the teacher had been giving the message of Alma found in chapter 5 of the book of Alma in the Book of Mormon. The discussion had not been active —the women seemed thoughtful, introspective, almost guilt ridden. At last the class leader said, "Sisters, let us ask ourselves what Alma asked his people. Have we experienced the mighty change? Is Christ's image reflected through us? Sisters, what of our countenances?"

The class wit, discouraged with self-improvement efforts, said, "What about paper bags?"

An Understanding Heart

King Solomon loved the Lord and the Lord loved Solomon. Solomon kept God's commandments, and he removed himself to a "great high place" called Gibeon, where he offered on the altar "a thousand burnt offerings." Following this period of seclusion and worship, the Lord appeared to Solomon and gave him what he asked for—"a wise and an understanding heart" with which to judge the people. The interesting thing is that God did this because Solomon had not asked for riches or for protection against enemies or for a long life. He had asked for qualities that would make him useful to people.

Insight! What of our own prayers? How much the quality of life would be improved, how much more love we'd enjoy in relationships, if we had understanding hearts!

Later two women came to Solomon for judgment. The biblical account says that the two lived together with no one else in the house. They delivered babies within a day or two of each other, but one baby died when its mother "overlaid" it in the night. This mother then quietly took the living baby and put her own dead baby in the arms of her friend. In the morning the friend recognized the dead baby as not her own, but the other woman stood fast in the lie. Finally they stood before King Solomon, told their respective versions of the happening, and waited for his judgment.

Solomon said, "Bring me a sword."

He determined to cut the child in two and give half to the one and half to the other woman. The natural mother was alarmed. She had a deep yearning for her son and loved him enough to plead that the king not slay the baby. The lying woman said, "Let it be neither mine nor thine, but divide it."

And wise King Solomon awarded the baby to its rightful, loving mother. (See 1 Kings 3.)

Insight. Love makes a difference in how we behave. For love's sake we sacrifice our own desires. King Solomon didn't ask God for self-serving desires. He asked to be useful to God's beloved children. And the loving mother cared more that her baby live than that she be allowed to mother him.

There are many moving examples of people who have made a personal sacrifice for a loved one. They run the gamut from laying down one's life for another to giving up a desired Christmas gift to a deprived neighbor.

As we grow in understanding of God's plans and purposes, and as our ability to love enough to meet the needs of others matures, how great it will be!

73

Family Love

There were forty family lines and as many different names brought into the gathering of one particular family (marriage quickly multiplies the possibilities, if one falls in love with a member of a large clan). Working at loving, accepting, and forgiving each other was part of their plan for peace. Who needs prosperity when you can have this kind of quality relationship?

It had been a time of reunion, and almost every cousin was there —the children of brothers and sisters who had grown older, now, but who loved each other the more because of the threat of time, and the richness of it, too. The longer a relationship lasts, the better it seems to get. Learning how to love and making a commitment to practice good loving is what families are all about.

We start with two, and we end with . . . !

Whatever their numbers, the goal of this family was to feel like hugging each other at the comings and the goings of the three-day reunion. It was to find and corner and talk in small groups. It was to sit in close quarters while reports were given to update activities among the family. It was to remember the dear members who had moved on to the next life. Thank God for the promise of continued sociality there! It was to promise to keep in touch as everyone scattered to homes far away or just down the block. It was to revel in family love—the closest thing to heaven on earth.

At the end of their time together this family was led in prayer by an uncle, and then they blended their voices and their hearts in a tender version of "God Be with You Till We Meet Again."

And it shall be so, because love works wonders.

74

Charity

The distinguished woman was old and frightened but faithful in attending church. She was walking to church one bright Sunday morning and was greeted by a neighbor hurrying to his meetings. She asked if she could take his arm to steady her walk to the chapel. He agreed and they took a few steps together. Then he begged good-bye and left her because he had to sit on the stand and didn't want to be late.

Where was charity?

The ''unusual'' cousin came to the funeral and moved among those gathered at the grave with equal, open friendliness for relative and stranger alike. Some moved away in distaste. Some visited for a moment then turned to others to talk. Yes, her talk was unusual and so was her clothing. Yes, her eyes shone too brightly and her walk was jerky. Her floppy hat and the bright daubs of pink on her cheeks bordered on the ludicrous.

But there was one who put an arm around her, pulling her close for a moment so as to spare her from an abrupt dismissal by a certain notable in the city.

There was charity.

We all come from heaven into the world—into the family, the ward, the neighborhood, the funeral or other special occasion—carrying our particular baggage. We have tendencies toward neatness or we don't. We have a sense of style or a lack of taste. Our nose grows too big, stays too small, flattens out, beaks or bulbs out of proportion with our face. Our chemistry runs amok. But here we come, and God tells us to love and be loved—to be charitable no matter what discomfort, inconvenience, or embarrassment this may cause.

We can count on being encircled in God's arms, but it's a tough world for any of us to get through if we can't count on each other's embraces as well.

A major ideal of the gospel seems to be that we should be ready to accept and pardon all others. It is our cheek we are to turn and our coat we are to give. Like the priest in *Les Misérables*, we give both candlesticks to the man caught stealing one. Robert Louis Stevenson suggested that when another's face is "buffeted, perhaps a little of the lion will become us best. That we are to suffer others to be injured and stand by is not conceivable and surely not desirable."

It is here that we are reminded of the classic statement on charity—or "the pure love of Christ"—as it is defined in the scriptures: it absolutely does not matter what else we are or have in all this world—including faith to move mountains—if we don't have charity, we are nothing.

How lovely a person Lucy Mack Smith must have been to come up with a thought like: "Let us all watch over each other, that we may sit down in heaven together."

Perfect Love?

Waiting for perfect love?

Making a switch in partners because you think you've found "perfect love"?

Forget it!

Perfect love? How so when there are no perfect people and it takes two of them to make "perfect love"?

Too many people have uttered such complaints as these: "I guess I never really loved you." "You aren't what I thought you'd be, at all." "This relationship was wrong from the beginning." "Is this all there is to married love?" "Time and eternity? I can hardly get through the day."

And off the disgruntled complainer trots to destroy a sacred alliance, break covenants, disrupt a family's finances, and hurt the hearts of the children—little and innocent, or grown-up and learning from example!

Perfect love is just a dream when a family hasn't learned to love beyond its borders: "Don't bring *that* girl into the family and expect me to love her like a daughter." "You'd better start praying for a different boyfriend—your father can never get along with this one."

Maybe perfect love isn't possible among imperfect people, but gratitude, obedience, and a recognition of the spark of the divine in each precious soul help make a more perfect love possible.

It's worth a try.

Small Moments of Love

The little things that keep us going in a kind of happiness, no matter what else is plaguing us in life, we call "small moments of love."

Why? Imagine! After twenty years . . . thirty . . . fifty . . . maybe only twenty grim minutes—after a long stretch of battle with adversity, some small, wonderful delight enters the scene. In that instant everything changes. Nothing has changed, but everything changes. We are quick to say, shout, declare, "All right! All right! Life *is* more than trouble! Life is an adventure! Love conquereth all. Hurrah!"

We exult over a small moment of love because it makes us feel *loved.*

Consider these possible ways of creating some small moments of love:

- a valentine from a big brother (seventy years old) with a lifting line, "How can anyone explain a sister like you—without bragging?" (to a sister equally old)
- a quote or a note of cheer ("Remember, you are a child of God.")
- a toy bank ("You can 'bank' on me!")
- a bundle of Guatemalan "worry dolls"
- an enormous heart cookie on Halloween (Who needs a witch when one is already in trouble?)
- a bag of golf tees with the tag, "Get away from it all with your ever-caring buddies."
- a candle, a light bulb, a flashlight, because the suffering friend is a bright light in life
- a garden bouquet, a single flower for Mom, Grandma, teacher, winner of the school election for Girls' Council
- a fat round loaf or an enormous sourdough baguette for the person who has cast so many loaves upon the water that it's time to get one back
- a corny but lovely cardboard crown, foil covered or crayon colored, emblazoned with the word *DAD*—the wearer receiving special attention all through that mealtime, at least
- a car wash and a poster on the day of Mom's Relief Society lesson, "Good luck, and tell them we love you!"

Surely the following incident has been repeated a time or two. The woman delivered a turkey and dressing to her neighbor struggling with a debilitating illness. The cook herself had only months to live.

"A burnt offering," she laughed, placing on the stove top the foil roaster pan filled with overdone turkey. "It's a tribute to you. I'm not much of a cook anymore, but I can still recognize courage when I see it."

A hug and a whisper, "I can't change anything but I can cry with you!"

In Shakespeare's play *Much Ado about Nothing,* Don Pedro says of his friend Benedick: "He hath a heart as sound as a bell, and his tongue is the clapper; for what his heart thinks his tongue speaks."[28] A kind word of warmth, approval, encouragement and a hug anytime, anyplace can slather a heart with hope, happiness, and can turn an ordinary time into a small moment of love.

Harvesting Love

The imagery of the farm is also known to city people, who may have no more to do with earth and growing things than to place a tomato plant in a pot in the window.

What you sow, you shall reap.

How often we have heard that truism, and in a variety of settings that have absolutely nothing to do with farming.

Plants bring forth their own fruit. Blessings follow the keeping of the laws upon which they are based. The scriptures underscore this idea for us in words found in the Doctrine and Covenants: "There is a law, irrevocably decreed in heaven before the foundations of this world, upon which all blessings are predicated—and when we obtain any blessing from God, it is by obedience to that law upon which it is predicated" (D&C 130:20–21).

In other words, if we want peaches we plant a peach tree. If we are after corn then we drop corn seed kernels into the ground.

If we want the blessing of a good marriage we keep the rules; we follow the guidelines that produce a good marriage.

If we want a friend we must be a friend.

And if we want to harvest love we must plant the seeds of love and cultivate, nourish, and be watchful. If we want to be loved, we must be loveable—that is, unless we are surrounded by good souls who already have learned God's lesson that we must love all people, regardless of what they choose to do about returning that love.

The parable of the sower (Matthew 13:18–23) is a powerful discourse on seeds and harvest. The application is to the word of God, but it works just as well for loving, for relationships of all kinds. There is a similar idea in Alma's missionary message (see Alma 32:28–41).

Let us make of our hearts a fertile ground ready to receive the seeds of affection, kindness, loyalty, great charity, or small love. Then the emotion we seek will grow and flourish. Accept with gratitude the love that comes our way and we will reap a fine crop of experiences and tender memories.

The Savior spoke of thorns and of the world's deceits that choke out the full benefit of the word of God growing within us. So it is with love.

John Hafen, a gifted artist at the turn of the century, made a suggestion to the viewers of his art show: "In paintings that you may see hereafter cease to look for mechanical effect or minute finish, for individual leaves, blades of grass, or aped imitation of things, but look for smell, for soul, for feeling, for the beautiful in color."

What sound advice for the person searching for solid relationships, some of them sweetened by romantic love, strengthened through marriage. In the matters of loving, why not cease to look to the minute finish of a person and instead look for soul, for feeling, for beauty. Why not consider the eternal possibilities of the person as well?

Then we will harvest love.

Honeycomb

Have you ever seen a wax honeycomb taken by a beekeeper out of a hive? Each cell is sealed off from the others and filled with its particular treasure. It is a thing of natural beauty.

The heart is a honeycomb to someone who has lived deeply. The various experiences of life—the hurts and joys alike—are sealed off from each other. Only then can survival and flourishing in personal growth happen.

How full of proverbial honey are the honeycombed hearts of people who love people and life! These are they who live richly, who are attuned to life's possibilities, who are sensitive to others —responsive to particular people in a particular way. These are they who are open to the feelings of gladness and sadness that inevitably come when one invests in life by taking risks, leaping in faith, caring more about others than self. These are they who have loved and lost and who have loved again by making adjustments in self, by dreaming another dream.

The idea of a honeycombed heart seems apropos to the kind of life we must learn to live here on earth. Seal up the experience that is over, and get on with life.

But there is more. Understanding the nature of life, we should remember to cherish each other in the recognition that we do not know how long we shall have each other—or how long we'll have a certain pleasurable assignment, or a certain association.

Promise and Realization

When Henry van Dyke wrote "Love Stays" for a garden sundial, he spoke a truth people discover for themselves as they mature in learning to love:

> Hours fly, flowers die.
> New days, new ways
> Pass by. Love stays.

And love does stay—if it is made welcome, if it is given generously and wisely, if each phase of life sees it grow and develop so that there is happiness and the making of memories that bring joy. From childish love for mother to the fulness of a good marriage, from friend-to-friend loyalty to warm brothers-in-the-gospel and sisters-in-the-circle relationships, love in its many aspects brings forth a more meaningful life.

There is the promise of love at any stage of life. The realization of love comes only as its price is paid. It will not come through madly pursuing it, nor is it based on selfishness or lust. We read in Moroni 7:48 that we should "pray unto the Father with all the energy of heart" that we might be filled with love. Energy! Now that is a valuable clue.

There is a time to feel each kind of love and a time and a way that are right for the expressions of it. There are qualities to cultivate in order to prepare oneself for the *highest* kind of feeling in any relationship.

In 1 Corinthians 13 we learn from Paul, a special disciple and agent of the Lord Jesus Christ, some valuable principles about love, principles which could be paraphrased as follows:

Pure love is patient,
　　long-suffering,
　　kind.
Pure love is not envious;
　　it does not boast;
　　it is not proud.
Pure love acts responsibly;
　　it is unselfish;
　　it is not easily provoked.
Pure love thinks virtuously;
　　it has no joy in evil but
　　rejoices in the truth.
Pure love is courageous,
　　faithful,
　　full of hope.
Pure love is steadfast.

Paul used the word *charity* as the name for the pure love of Christ. In a similar passage of scripture, the Nephite prophet Mormon spoke of charity. He went on to say, "It endureth forever; and whoso is found possessed of it at the last day, it shall be well with him" (Moroni 7:47).

And with *her,* too.

May it, indeed, be well with us all at that day that draws ever nearer.

Love Is a Verb

Love is a verb. It can be a quiet feeling in the heart, but the best love is shared and shown. Both the one loved and the one loving benefit from the joy that happens when something wonderful is done out of love—for one particular loved one or for the human race. Love should be considered an action word, with people moving out to spread joy in today's world.

Bear each other's burdens, the gospel teaches, and we come to love God more. We learn that his principles, given to us to live our lives by, work. They really work!

Jesus said to feed his sheep. We can teach, nudge, comfort, nurture, guide, humor and josh, show by example, explain and testify of God's goodness. We can do this in appropriate ways with any of God's children who cross our path. Keep an open eye for opportunities, and it will come to pass.

Love thy neighbor, the scriptures say again and again. We've seen the frazzled mother in the supermarket yank the arm of her small child. We want to yank hers back. One thinks of minding one's own business. But that child is our neighbor, too. Minding one's business is a virtue, but what about moving in to console the mother and receive her complaints and then compliment her on her child. Something like, "Children can wear a person down to the nub, can't they? But a bright one [a pretty one, a lively one, and so forth] like this one is worth it. You are blessed! Fear not!"

Wasn't it Anne Morrow Lindbergh who said that her life couldn't implement in action all the demands on her heart? Well, perhaps, but with God nothing is impossible—even responding in action (however small) when a drop of love can change the chemistry.

Action doesn't mean big, complicated, expensive, elaborate, time-consuming, and energy-sapping endeavors. Love in action can be the kind word or the sincere smile, the brief touch of a hand on the arm, eye to eye contact, a prayer for guidance.

Needs are great among people today. And though we have to learn to face our own trials,—with God, if we're wise—the healing balm of company is a blessing in time of misery, anger, temptation. Supporting others is a way of loving.

Christ's love shining through others brings newness to life. The Apostle Paul said, "Be ye kind one to another" (Ephesians 4:32). *Kind* is another word for *love*.

81

Love Is a Great Idea

Science can't find a cure for the common cold, so we go on sniffling and sharing remedies.

Science has, however, discovered countless other things—ways for filling time, having fun, staying well, repairing the body, training the mind, cleaning the house, writing down the spoken word, recording it on cassette, crossing the earth's surface by land, sea, or air. There is endless, amazing variety in the gadgets that science has provided to do everything for us, including brushing our teeth.

Science has not come up with a method for expressing love that is better than what God gave us. It is left for us to do what machines can't—love each other, for instance. Computers can take the option out of dating but not the excitement out of the heart of the girl, or the hope out of the heart of the boy.

Let us learn to love each other. Let us learn to give love to others whether they return the feeling or not. We will be better for the giving. We will be keeping God's commandments, and following his will is the best way to live. Loving does much to overcome the haunted loneliness Emily Dickinson wrote about. Self-pity gets us no place. Self-worship in the form of consumerism and the pursuit of pleasure ends up like a wad of cotton in the mouth. We really can't hug that boat in bed!

People learn at a pace different from each other. The person we choose to love may not understand how keenly we desire to be loved in return. But if we approach a relationship with the mature, educated-heart point of view (giving, loving, giving), in time the other person may learn. As we already have!

Part of loving is waiting—patiently, if possible. Looking for paybacks or for the fulfillment of precious expectations is futile. Love comes at its own time. People get perfect *someday!*

Giving up on others too soon can bring unhappiness and the severing of a fine relationship. It can even bring divorce. President Spencer W. Kimball stunned the congregation in the Salt Lake Tabernacle when he affirmed that "divorce is spelled S-E-L-F-I-S-H-N-E-S-S."[29]

Part of loving is loving *anyway*. God loves us not because we are responsive to his love, grateful for his love, or even recognize his love; God loves us because *he* is good, not because we are. The promise, the direction, the hope of all of life is that we become like him. We *become* by *being!* Way to go . . . hmmm?

Over a hundred years ago Elder John Taylor reminded the good people in his day that love is a great idea—a way to garner the blessings of the Lord. He said: "Let husbands love their wives, and be full of kindness towards them. Let wives study their husbands, and with kindness seek to make a heaven for them, that love and happiness may reign in our habitations. Let parents teach their children both by precept and example, the virtues of Gospel truths, that they may grow up in the love and fear of God, and that you may be the blessed of the Lord, and your offspring with you."[30]

Love is a great idea. It has always been a great idea. It would be well if we'd try this great idea. If the idea of love is accepted, it remains for us to find ways to carry it out.

The Unveiling

In the community park the covering is dropped from the new sculpture, and people gasp in delight as the work of the artist is revealed.

In the quiet of the holy place—wherever custom, religion, or preference demand marriage should happen—traditionally the bride is veiled. She removes her veil as the ceremony uniting the couple is completed. This is an ancient tradition. It suggests keeping one's secrets secret until one chooses to give herself to her husband. It is symbolic of virtue, of vulnerability, and thus the bride needs the protection of her husband. It is symbolic of giving more than body; it is a reminder that the woman gives her soul, too, by revealing, by becoming known, by showing and telling, "This is who I am. Take me, as is!"

Not only "take me," we might add, but also "cherish me."

This tradition of unveiling can help us learn about our relationship with God. We should remove the veil, not because he can't see beneath the veil, but because it is important for us to yield to him, to relax a stiff neck and a proud demeanor.

We reveal self to our Heavenly Father, to our Creator, who has known us from the beginning. We humble ourselves in doing this. We admit our weaknesses, we own up to our awareness that we're not yet what God wants us to be. We confess our sins. We plead for forgiveness and for help!

Now we have opened the channel for God to both help us and preserve our agency. He loves us, but do we love him enough to trust him by placing the open book of our life before him?

Friends and Enemies

We hear a song and our heart melts. We think of someone well loved so long ago. The feeling is still there! It surfaces by a chance hearing of melody!

A scent in the air makes our breath catch . . . can it be? No, just the scent on a stranger or a free sample in the cosmetic department as we walk on by. Yet for us that fragrance is tied to a person we used to love—love still, apparently, even though the relationship is over.

Quite by chance one day we read something like the following lines from Rupert Brooke: "And the hawthorn hedge puts forth its buds, / And my heart puts forth its pain." We relish the agony of remembered love. Pain is a part of loving, but making enemies never should be. For love remembered is still its own wonderful reward.

There are in the world so many worthwhile people to care about, to like and enjoy, to find affinity with, even to put on your prayer list—to love with Godlike love, so to speak, without aching of passion.

For a moment, see the faces, say the names in your mind.

The favorite teacher, the beloved departed baby-sitter, the hearty and helpful storekeeper, the counselor we visited in time of trouble, the neighbor who welcomed someone else's pets and children and endured trampled flower beds, the personal friend we've loved since childhood.

These were choice people . . . easy to love.

But how about—shall we say it?—the not-so-choice ones with obnoxious personality traits? Can they be loved?

Can we love the mechanic (or whomever) who cheated us on car repairs?

Can we love the absolutely tiresome acquaintance who demands so much attention; who, when a smile is given, assumes intimacy exists between us; who demands time, energy, a listening ear?

Can we go on loving the child who is defiant regarding family standards; who is in constant trouble with school authorities and the law; who is obviously in deep trouble and is a plague on parental energy? Can we?

We aren't talking just God's commandments to love all men, here, we're talking making life more pleasant for ourselves as well as others. Why be miserable in relationships, when we can look for something to appreciate, to love about someone else?

Fact: We want to be forgiven for our shortcomings—carelessness, overweight, thoughtlessness, bossiness and busyness, judging, and so on. We want to be loved, appreciated, regarded highly, recognized (call it what you will).

The Savior's word: "And as ye would that men should do to you, do ye also to them likewise. For if ye love them which love you, what thank have ye? for sinners also love those that love them." (Luke 6:31–32.)

These are great lines. But wait a minute. Now we're not only to love the cheating mechanic; we're also to love our enemies—the person who spreads false rumors, keeps us out of Rotary, poisons our pets! We're not only to love our fellowmen; we're also supposed to look at the broad picture and find something admirable, acceptable—well, tolerable—about "the mechanic" or whomever. Life is too short to have unpleasant relationships. It is too long for hating.

Conclusion: We are supposed to be better than sinners.

We are supposed to polish our good points, eliminate the questionable traits in ourselves, and ever move toward perfection, exaltation, and forever happiness. God's rules and his will are for our good. What can be good about loving our enemy? He ceases to be an enemy, that's what! He ceases to cause the soul to sour, at least.

We can learn to love our enemies by heeding the all-important counsel and secret of success given to us by our Creator. "I say unto you which hear, Love your enemies, do good to them which hate you, bless them that curse you, and pray for them which despitefully use you" (Luke 6:27–28).

This is our charge. And though an enemy, an angry family member, disgruntled repairman—or, on the grander scale, a nation—may disregard our teachings or scoff at our friendly efforts, it is still our commission to love our enemies and other unpleasant people about us.

Each of us can show Godlike love to his enemies by being "an example of the believers," as Paul declared to Timothy. Paul went on to give instruction about how to do this. He said that one should be an example "in word, in conversation, in charity, in spirit, in faith, in purity." (1 Timothy 4:12.)

What a giant step forward toward peace, even heaven on earth! What a boost in our personal progress toward becoming even as Christ is!

Love's Divine Nature

Grace and peace
be multiplied unto you
through the
knowledge of
God,
and of
Jesus our Lord. . . .
Be partakers of the divine nature,
having escaped the corruption
that is in the world
through lust.
And beside this,
giving all diligence,
add to your
faith virtue;
and to
virtue knowledge;
and to
knowledge temperance;
and to
temperance patience;
and to

patience godliness;
and to
godliness brotherly kindness;
and to
brotherly kindness charity.
(See 2 Peter 1:2, 4–7.)

Love Learned

Every era of struggle among mankind on earth has its stories of love amidst hate. Where man hasn't grown up in God there have been inquisitions, holocausts, religious uprisings, mobbings, hostage taking, lynchings, murders, and unrighteous dominion.

Every country has its shame. Every generation carries guilt. If ever we were to harness the power of love and use it for the good of all men, then, indeed, could come the Millennium.

It is heartening to know that there are so many great stories of love in history. Here is one that happened in the early part of the twentieth century, during the course of the Armenian atrocities.

A Turkish soldier chased a young woman and her brother down an alley where he cornered them in an angle of the wall, and the brother was slain before his sister's eyes. She dodged down the alley, leaped a wall, and escaped.

Later, being a nurse, she was forced by the Turkish authorities to work in the military hospital. One day into her ward was brought that same Turkish soldier who had slain her brother. He was very ill. A slight inattention would ensure his death. The young woman later admitted to the bitter struggle that took place in her mind and heart. Her natural self cried, "Vengeance!" and her better, Christian self cried, "Love!" The better side of her conquered. She nursed him as carefully as any other patient in the ward.

The recognition was mutual, and one day, unable to restrain his curiosity, the Turk asked his nurse why she had not let him die.

She replied, "I am a follower of him who said, 'Love your enemies and do them good.' "

He was silent for a long time. At last he spoke, "I never knew that there was such a philosophy. If that is your religion, tell me more about it, for I want it."

Love can be learned. And God has promised us that if we live in peace, then the God of love and peace will be with us.

Where Love Is

Among the countless number of volumes about love there are expressions about loving and losing; about fulfillment and rejection; about dying love; about dying *in* love; about physical love and examples of pure spiritual love; about the pain and pleasure of romance; about the satisfaction in unselfish, affectionate giving; about the heights the soul can reach when God is part of a relationship.

In this book the collection of expressions includes a wide perspective on the subject of love. But these aren't mere poems, stories, scriptures, definitions, considerations—even motivations. They aren't just rose thorns or love pricks to make you feel better when you read the stuff. Though even that might be reason enough to consider them.

These expressions, it is hoped, help the reader to be thoughtful about a love, about a generous experience of the heart, about a neighborly assistance or a compassionate service, about a love withheld in love, or about enduring and sacrificing in love.

For us, imperfect as we are, we can either love or try to love until we do. In love, practice makes perfect.

We may not have read Shakespeare in grade school. So, in a series of small deeds and simple expressions we build a basis for grand loving. Where love is, there God is also, for God is love. Learning to treat people as the Lord would is rewarding and right, whether it is a romantic alliance or a parental or neighborly relationship.

Love is not getting but it is giving.

Love isn't fantasies of desire, demanding fulfillment. Even romantic love requires giving of self.

Love isn't a throbbing of the heart, glistening of the eyes, restlessness of being. These may be there, but there is more than that to true love.

Love is spiritual fire. It is goodness, generosity, and graciousness. Love is refinement of the body and spirit. It is peace and wholesome living. Remember the famous lines by P. J. Bailey:

> Ask not of me, love, what is love?
> Ask what is good of God above—
> Ask of the great sun what is light—
> Ask what is darkness of the night.

One thing we know, love stays. The expression of it may change and the description of it remain elusive, but love stays. You see, God is love, and God is eternal.

Moral Love

You've heard about the fools who rush in where angels fear to tread? Well, it seems to be happening everywhere one looks these days. But right and wrong are not based on the number of people acting like fools or angels. Moral love is still based on God's commandment.

God is good, whether any of us is or not.

God's counsel is still eternal counsel, whether we apply it to our lives or not. News media, entertainment trends, fashion gimmicks do not a commandment make.

Moral love is the most gratifying love because it is according to God's will. Satan is ruler over the quick satisfaction, the fast thrill, the gratification of the moment. Cheap price, cheap result.

Moral love has to do with love of God, love of self, love of others. It is the only way to go.

Loving God means keeping his commandments. So he says!

Loving self means keeping God's commandments for our own good, our own happiness, our own eternal position, our peace and quiet conscience now. Loving self means respect of the spark of the divine that is in each of us. Some people may not know this—yet! But you do.

Loving others means you don't play the immoral love game and be an instrument in messing up someone else's life. Back off!

Whether we are old or young, married or single, we are drawn to some people more than others. But to start building a new nest on top of another—to "play married"—is not only hurtful and a sin; it's unnecessary. Isn't being friends enough?

Moods of Love

It seems there has always been a preoccupation with love in every culture and in every time, so there are many voices and moods of love. Incredibly and delightfully, love is the language and the emotion that is understood across time and place among all of God's children.

Robert Frost said that earth was the right place for love. "I don't know where it's likely to go better!"

Earth as we know it came about thanks to Adam and Eve using their agency to share in the search for knowledge, to make choices, to discern the difference between right and wrong. To progress! Do you remember Milton's lines about their love, included in his masterpiece *Paradise Lost?*

At one point, Adam addresses Eve silently in his mind:

> O fairest of Creation, last and best
> Of all God's Works, Creature in whom excell'd
> Whatever can to sight or thought be form'd,
> Holy, divine, good, amiable, or sweet![31]

Then aloud to her he says, in part, these powerful words:

> So forcible within my heart I feel
> The Bond of Nature draw me to my own,
> My own in thee, for what thou art is mine;
> Our State cannot be sever'd, we are one,
> One Flesh; to lose thee were to lose myself.[32]

Emily Dickinson wrote of love in many of its facets, through various levels of feeling. Her lines "Love is life—and life hath Immortality" have been rephrased by poets ever since and used to define this Godlike emotion called love.

> That I did always love
> I bring the Proof
> That till I loved
> I never lived—Enough—
>
> That I shall love alway—
> I argue thee
> That love is life—
> And life hath Immortality—

A man asked that I use the following words of Herrick in the funeral sermon for his young wife. He said that she had made him what he was (and it was good!) by being his eyes, his ears, his heart in his work, in his service to God, and in his relationships with others.

> Thou art my life, my love, my heart,
> The very eyes of me;
> Thou hast command of every part
> To live and die for thee.

We live in times where proof is required before belief can settle in the heart. What's more, some take to lustful ways and care little for the ideal of pure, true love as the power behind intimate expression.

It is mistakenly thought that to make oneself vulnerable, exposed to the possibility of hurt or mental cruelty (as they call it in the courts), is too high a price to pay for sharing sacred life with another.

But surely there is something to be said for romantic, ecstatic love and Godlike appreciation of each other.

Some search madly through the works of the masters to find expression high enough to describe such great emotion. Charles Swain, in his lines "I Will Tell Thee What It Is to Love," writes that to love is "to build with human thoughts a shrine, / Where Hope sits brooding like a beauteous dove; / Where Time seems young, and Life a thing divine. / All tastes, all pleasures, all desires combine / To consecrate this sanctuary of bliss / . . . the best, the brightest boon the heart e'er knew: / Of all life's sweets the very sweetest yet!"

Of course, it is better to have loved and lost than never to have loved at all!

But, perhaps, one needs to have lived a lot of years to witness the truth of that statement. I am thankful that I have. To whatever youthful romantics there are who may not believe it yet, I suggest Edna St. Vincent Millay's romantic verse:

> I cannot say what loves have come and gone;
> I only know that summer sang in me
> A little while, that in me sings no more.

Well, as many mothers and fathers have insisted across the years to a disappointed, swooning, heartbroken, loveless youth in the family: There are, indeed, other fish in the ocean, other sand on the shore, other daisy blooms in the field. Give love another try. Go and bring joy, do kind deeds, reach to understand other nice people, and one day . . .

89

Quiet Gladness of the Soul

These lines by Ina Draper Defoe were quoted by Ted Malone over fifty years ago on his popular radio show. And they are still good. (Do any of you remember Ted Malone?)

Autumn, be kind to her, slow your arrival;
Summer, be good to her, let the revival
Of Spring in her body be passionate, heady;
Love may yet come to her, let her be ready.

This thought may be more relevant today, the statistics on single people being what they are. Single girls, no longer truly young and caught in a trend, hope for a day of love . . . one day . . .

Everything changes. Nothing changes. The loves of the past can still stir your heart—even if they have little to do with the present. Some nameless genius with an understanding of life and love wrote the lines that follow. They point up the far reach and the other face of love. People can be drawn together but still resist "nest building" on top of an "already built nest," you see.

Did you ever go back to the woman you used to love, after it was all over—the heartaches, the self-conflict, the numbness, and all that—to find in her a friend who understood, whose spirit had grown sweeter, finer, truer than it used to be in the old days when you loved but did not understand how beautiful is such a friendship, and how rare?

There is a tenderness between you, a sincerity of truth, a subtle bond of union infinitely greater in its strength and firmness than the old-time passion ever bore. It isn't love as the world sees it, it doesn't ruffle you or make you blind; there is no swift and frequent alteration of ecstasy and despair; no jealousy, or intoxication of the senses, but just peace and natural sympathy, and a subtle, quiet gladness of the soul. You never quite forget her, even though you meet another woman and marry her for love. There is always the fragrant memory of the other woman, whom you loved and lost, and found again in a friend who understood.

"Subtle, quiet gladness of the soul" . . . now, isn't that nice? Mature affection, grown-up loving, has its own reward.

It seems needful sometimes, as we are looking back across our lives—in the spirit of gratitude to God and friends—to send a message to one we have loved.

Wherever that person might be in all the world, to whatever position of worth and honor he might have risen, however many babies she might have had, it is an act of gratitude to remember that we *are* what we have *felt* and what we have *shared* with a friend. There is too much that we give each other in a relationship that goes beyond the trappings of loving. All the rest of life is blessed by the beauty, the pain, the accommodation of other's needs and tendencies, the way life and problems and hopes are seen, what goals are set. When comfort, encouragement, and loveliness have been shared once, why not speak again in gratitude across the years in an act worthy of a child of God?

Peaceable Things

Even the phrase "peaceable things" settles one's mind right down. For a moment the angry hassle of the institutional world disappears in the consideration of peace and love and contentment.

Blue-sky talk, you say? Ah, but God says it is possible. And through God all things *are possible*—love in place of loneliness, fulfillment in place of frustration, peace in place of turmoil.

Regardless of the world—regardless, even, of others in a room —there can be peaceable things in your life!

Such an idea comes by good authority—the word of God. We learn in Doctrine and Covenants 39:6 that the Holy Ghost *teaches* the peaceable things of the kingdom. Love is one of the peaceable things. Such a coveted condition! One cultivates the companionship of the Holy Ghost, heeds its promptings, and thus draws from this source guidance and power to improve personal relationships in life.

All right! But there is more . . .

It is startling to come across a scripture like the one that concludes section 130 of the Doctrine and Covenants. This verse declares that a person may receive the Holy Ghost, and it may descend upon that person, and yet not tarry. What is implied here is the doctrine with which we each should be familiar—that the Holy Ghost is able to function (to teach, comfort, warn, enhance, witness, and so on) only in an element of purity and faith.

The Spirit prompts us to do a loving act, a particular good. Our prayers for guidance put us into a position to follow through. Proving helpful to our perspective are the examples among ancient prophets in the long history of mankind. There is good material to live by in the book of Ezekiel, and on this subject of love, particularly, verses 31 and 32 of Ezekiel 33 are pertinent: "And they come unto thee as the people cometh, and they sit before thee as my people, and they hear thy words, but they will not do them: for with their mouth they shew much love, but their heart goeth after their covetousness. And, lo, thou art unto them as a very lovely song of one that hath a pleasant voice, and can play well on an instrument: for they hear thy words, but they do them not."

May we strive to become more pure and full of faith; may we be wise and not only hear the word of God but also do it, that we may know love and the peaceable things.

Self-Love

And what of love of self? Consideration, at least? We really can't love others until we value our place in the kingdom of God, recognize our relationship to him and, therefore, to all mankind. What an ego booster is the knowledge that our dear Lord loves us all the same!

When you grow up reciting classic lines such as those that follow here, you are given a great perspective for decision making. One wants to make that little person in the baby picture proud. When you have recited them sixty jillion times, as I have, in public talks to the youth of several generations, the sense of value in such questioning is driven home to the heart.

> So You were I . . .
> Somehow.
> I can't think thru
> To that forgotten time
> When I was You.
> Could your clear eyes
> Read
> What is in my own,
> Would You
> Feel disappointment
> At the Me
> To which
> You've grown?

The mother of a brood of toddlers and preschoolers was the speaker at the youth meeting in church. And while she spoke the father hustled a squawking new infant out of the chapel. The "brood" of little people followed promptly after him. They clung about his legs while he tried, unsuccessfully, to pacify the baby.

At last it was over. For the rest of the meeting both mother and father tussled with their offspring—the fruit of their loving.

When Mother came into the hall, the father complained about "tot-tending" during the meeting. He felt forgotten, put upon, unloved.

He was not "tot-tending," the young mother explained to the young father. How could he be a tot-tender? That's hired help. These children were his as well as hers!

Later at home, as the couple talked, they comforted, nourished, expressed appreciation, felt deep gratitude, too, assured and reassured. They validated each other. They loved and urged each other to love themselves as they did each other.

Tots to tend, babies to bear notwithstanding, they were individuals who needed love from each other but who also needed to love themselves enough to feel secure until such love could be forthcoming.

God can't be with us every second, either, patting us on the head, showering us with grandiose, visible blessings. But we know him, and therefore we know that he loves us always and forever as we go about our life's work. Meanwhile, we mock God and we are ungrateful if we don't love ourselves as members of his family.

92

Love for God

There is a promise, made anciently to the humble and the obedient, that has been repeated over the generations among God's children: He will love us and bless us; he will multiply us and bless the fruit of the womb, as well as the fruit of our land and flocks.

He will love us, and we love him, too.

Praise God, from whom all blessings flow! How can we not love him when he has given us such wonderful blessings of:

— personal love
— family

— gospel principles to make life more pleasant and trials more bearable and eternity more than a promise
— comforts and comfort
— amenities
— adventures
— protection
— support
— knowing that he slumbers not nor sleeps but watches over us day and night
— drawing near to us when we draw near to him

Praise God. Love God. Lift eyes to the blessings of beauty about us.

His creations are magnificent and beyond telling:

— the chasing ripples of a mountain stream
— Vermont countryside in autumn with crayons of trees
— red outcroppings, white cliffs, sage bluffs, blue mountain ranges in the Grand Circle of southern Utah
— incredible heaven, clouds and colorings, of Rocky Mountain big sky country
— palm-threaded, ocean-mirrored Hawaiian sunsets
— myriad flowers, foliage, fruit, vegetables
— mornings in summer, glistening stars in winter
— baby anything!

Praise God for miracles:

— "built-in" directions to spawning salmon, carrier pigeons, migrating birds
— the workings of the human hands
— the conception, development, and birth of a baby
— the infusion of the spirit into the body of man

Love God? Show that love by keeping all his commandments with increasing devotion as we grow toward perfection?

Yes. The reward is to be "encircled about eternally in the arms of his love" (2 Nephi 1:15) and, meanwhile, to feel a unique sweetness, warmth, flooding of light and security, and well-being.

Loveable

Well, now, who among us doesn't want to be loved? And all the time, whether we deserve it or not. There is firm proof that if a person wants to be loved, to be a beloved, he or she must be loveable. We can't trust, you see, that the object of our affection is a firm believer in or a practitioner of God's counsel that we love all people.

This is not an essay on virtue and vice, strength and weakness, beauty and character. It is a reminder that love happens sometimes, ready or not. And while we are influenced by the company we keep and the direction our heart pours, we may recognize that love can surmount physical handicap, personality flaws, rather ordinary mentality and appearance.

Loveableness is an asset, however. It enhances any relationship. It is worth working for.

I read something by D. H. Lawrence that seems especially remarkable and suitable for consideration on this subject: "All I ask of a woman is that she feel gently towards me. When my heart feels kindly toward her there shall be the soft, soft tremor of unheard bells between us. It is all I ask. I am so tired of violent women lashing out and insisting on being loved when there is no love in them."

Bravo!

Study material for such a project of becoming more loveable should include Elizabeth Barrett Browning's "How Do I Love Thee?" There are very good clues there. And the love writings of Ella Wheeler Wilcox, William Robert Spencer, Robert Burns, Thomas Moore, John Donne, Christina Rossetti, William Makepeace Thackeray, and William Wordsworth. Don't forget the Gospel of John, and the expressions of Ecclesiastes about there being a time and season for every purpose under heaven—good clues there, as well. For pure love, deepest emotional love, turn to 3 Nephi 17 in the Book of Mormon.

You will weep as Christ did, as the multitudes did. Hearts changed, and the people loved and were loveable.

Remember, one doesn't fall into pure love or Godlike love. One reaches up to it. To love as God loves is to believe in the spark of the divine in all men and to value God's gifts or principles for relating to others. This is a major step toward becoming loveable.

94

How to Love

Is not life a thousand times too brief for us to only tolerate each other?

The ways of love are endless. There are different kinds of love, this we all know. But all stem from caring about someone else more than self and responding appropriately, generously, speedily.

Expressions of love vary with the situation. Such variety appears endless, too—from nose rubs with baby to a kissed finger going from Grandma to the cheek of a teenage grandson who has had his long hair cut off (at last!) for the mission field; from a neighbor warming a new family with a surprise cleaning of the snow-packed driveway to the missionary who learns to love unconditionally his strange companion (who thinks *he* is strange in return!) by making a list of his companion's good points and making a point of listing them before the younger elder does.

We are to learn about endless love, the charity that never disappears but always will be, even after all other things have passed away, as the scriptures remind us. Charity is Christ's love for us. If we are to become like him, then we must begin to learn to love as he does. He abhors the sin, of course, but he loves the sinner—the tiresome, the weak, and the arrogant, strong types, too. So must we. We begin by beginning!

Counting blessings. Noting the positive qualities of the other person. Complimenting. Doing a kindness. Sharing. Surprising. Delighting. And at last sacrificing for the happiness or well-being of another.

Marvelous stories of love can come from times of war, depression, extreme trauma in earthquake or flood. They may arise out of tragic situations—a child is lost in the wilderness; a young father is killed; a neighbor girl is abused; a mother dies; the bishop's house burns; immigrants need a doctor. The spirit of love is manifest in many ways—a new temple is being built and humble people donate nearly three times the needed amount!

How does one begin to love? How does one begin to be generous of heart, to have a supportive spirit?

Remember that each of us has not only different talents but also different ways of loving. Each special brand of love will touch someone whom another brand can't quite move. To live, inspire, warm, and comfort as best we can is the way to go.

Start. Begin. Try. Go for it.

Pray for strength and softness to do God's will in loving. It isn't romantic love we're speaking of here, is it? But romantic love—if it moves forward correctly—changes into precious charitable love that is even more satisfying, if we pray for strength to do what is right and softness to accept and love until the process is completed.

We get our hearts and our minds under control—focused on the great commandment (given to us for our own good!) to love God and all men.

In a world with endowments listed in programs, names etched on bronze plaques, it is sweetly sobering to hear one family explain their anonymous good deeds this way: "We want to remain anonymous. If people don't know the giver, then that night their prayer of thanksgiving will be to God, the source of all good gifts."

Love Defined

There are many definitions of love; the entire collection of thoughts in this book is loved defined. But following are some scriptural insights.

Love: "God is love" (1 John 4:16). That is, the fulness of love's possibilities and perfections are embodied in God the Father and Jesus Christ. The power of love taken into our own lives changes us and we become ever more like them. Love is

- *comforting*—"Be faithful and diligent in keeping the commandments of God, and I will encircle thee in the arms of my love" (D&C 6:20).
- *joyous*—"No one can conceive of the joy which filled our souls at the time we heard [Jesus] pray for us unto the Father. . . . And he said unto [the multitude]: Blessed are ye because of your faith. And now behold, my joy is full. And when he had said these words, he wept." (3 Nephi 17:17, 20–21.)

- *forgiving*—"Be ye kind one to another, tenderhearted, forgiving one another, even as God for Christ's sake hath forgiven you" (Ephesians 4:32).
- *likeminded*—"Fulfil ye my joy, that ye be likeminded, having the same love, being of one accord, of one mind" (Philippians 2:2).
- *compassionate*—"Be ye all of one mind, having compassion one of another, love as brethren, be pitiful, be courteous" (1 Peter 3:8).
- *gentle*—"But we were gentle among you, even as a nurse cherisheth her children: so being affectionately desirous of you, we were willing to have imparted unto you, not the gospel of God only, but also our own souls, because ye were dear unto us" (1 Thessalonians 2:7–8).
- *all-conquering*—"Neither death, nor life, nor angels, nor principalities, nor powers, nor things present, nor things to come, nor height, nor depth, nor any other creature, shall be able to separate us from the love of God, which is in Christ Jesus our Lord" (Romans 8:38–39).
- *pure*—"Charity is the pure love of Christ, and it endureth forever; and whoso is found possessed of it at the last day, it shall be well with him. . . . Pray unto the Father with all the energy of heart, that ye may be filled with this love . . . that when he shall appear we shall be like him . . . that we may be purified even as he is pure." (Moroni 7:47–48.)

"Love," wrote Henry Drummond nearly a hundred years ago, "is the *summum bonum.*" He got the idea from studying the scriptures. Jesus taught that upon love of God, love of others, and love of self "hang all the law and the prophets" (Matthew 22:37–40). The Apostle Paul wrote: "For all the law is fulfilled in one word, even in this; Thou shalt love thy neighbor as thyself" (Galatians 5:14).

96

A New Commandment

We all know the message of the Savior about love. He told us to love each other as ourselves. He told us that it was easy to love people we liked, but we should also love our enemies and those that persecute us. Some expectation! And we should love each other always. That means no matter what. Jesus "loved his own which were in the world," and "he loved them unto the end." And he loved them no matter what they did.

He loved Judas enough to hand him the *sop of esteem and friendship* during the Last Supper.

He loved Peter enough to forgive him for denying him three times. And he asked him to feed his lambs and his sheep—his Saints.

He loved John enough to allow him to tarry without death until the Second Coming.

And he loved us all enough to lay down his life for us, that those who believe in him might have eternal life.

The account in John 13 describing Jesus washing the feet of his disciples is wondrous. Sandaled feet on dusty streets were filthy. This scene is touching, tender, significant; it is what love on all levels is about. Here Jesus offered a precious example of love. After washing their feet he said to the disciples, "I have given you an example, that ye should do as I have done to you." He was trying to teach them that if he, their Master, was essentially their servant, then they should be servants to one another. If we love someone we are to serve him.

Husbands, wives, children, parents, teachers, bosses, employees, committee members, neighbors—hear this! Make things pleasant for each other. Stand by and weep for each other if there is nothing at the moment you can do, no other way in which you can serve. This is what Christ is teaching, it seems to me. This is the way to heart warmth, satisfaction, elation of spirit, no more loneliness or self-pity. It is in fact a reflection of the sacred ceremony of Christ washing the feet of his disciples.

"Now before the feast of the passover, when Jesus knew that his hour was come that he should depart out of this world unto the Father, having loved his own which were in the world, he loved them unto the end. And supper being ended, . . . he riseth from supper, and laid aside his garments; and took a towel, and girded himself. After that he poureth water into a bason, and began to wash the disciples' feet, and to wipe them with the towel wherewith he was girded." And then, not long after this, Jesus said to them: "A new commandment I give unto you, That ye love one another."

And Christ also promised on that occasion that if a person will love him and will keep his words, the Father will love that person, and together the Father and the Son will come unto that person and, he said, "make our abode with him" (John 14:23).

There is the essence of love.

We begin with basics, with serving. We continue in good works, in loving as Christ loved. We end as companions with God.

Notes

1. Gordon B. Hinckley, " 'This Work Will Go Forward,' " *Ensign* 20 (November 1990): 5.

2. Quoted in Helen Exley, ed., *Thank Heavens for Friends!* (Watford, England: Exley Publications, 1986).

3. Quoted in Exley, *Thank Heavens for Friends!*

4. Antoine de Saint-Exupéry, *The Little Prince*, trans. Katherine Woods (New York: Harcourt, Brace and World, 1943), pp. 65–67.

5. Mary Webb, *Precious Bane* (1924; reprint, New York: Penguin Books, 1989), pp. 94–96.

6. *Precious Bane,* p. 271.

7. Kahlil Gibran, *The Prophet* (New York: Alfred A. Knopf, 1923), pp. 15–16.

8. See Anne Morrow Lindbergh, *Gift from the Sea* (New York: Pantheon Books, 1955), pp. 104–6.

9. David Cory, "Miss You," in Hazel Felleman, sel., *The Best Loved Poems of the American People* (Garden City, New York: Doubleday, 1936), p. 42.

10. Carol Haynes, "Any Wife or Husband," in Felleman, *Best Loved Poems*, p. 23.

11. Leigh Hunt, "Jenny Kissed Me," in Felleman, *Best Loved Poems*, p. 6.

12. Anne Morrow Lindbergh, *War Within and Without: Diaries and Letters of Anne Morrow Lindbergh, 1939–1944* (New York: Harcourt Brace Jovanovich, 1980), pp. 421–22.

13. From *Teachers Who Touch Lives*, Horizon Publishers, P. O. Box 490, Bountiful, UT 84011-0490. Compiled by Philip L. Barlow; from the chapter "Perceptive Gentleness" by Ken Godfrey, p. 118.

14. Alan Jay Lerner, "I Loved You Once in Silence," from act 2, scene 6 of *Camelot* (New York: Random House, 1961), p. 103, italics added.

15. Lindbergh, *Gift from the Sea*, pp. 108–9.

16. S. W. R., "A Perfect Squelch," *Reader's Digest*, September 1990, p. 82.

17. *History of the Church* 4:606–7.

18. Brigham Young, in *Journal of Discourses* 3:361.

19. George A. Smith, in *Journal of Discourses* 12:25.

20. Quoted in Spencer J. Palmer, *The Expanding Church* (Salt Lake City: Deseret Book Co., 1978), p. v.

21. Maureen Derrick Keeler, "Discovering God's Love," *Ensign* 12 (April 1982): 11.

22. See Bible Dictionary, LDS edition of the Bible, p. 648.

23. *Teachings of the Prophet Joseph Smith*, sel. Joseph Fielding Smith (Salt Lake City: Deseret Book Co., 1938), p. 241.

24. *Webster's New World Dictionary* (New York: Simon and Schuster, 1990), s.v.

25. Joseph Devlin, *A Dictionary of Synonyms and Antonyms* (New York: Warner Books, 1987), s.v.

26. Allen E. Bergin, "The Way to Christlike Love," *Ensign* 12 (December 1982): 55.

27. See Lawrence Elliott, "Legend of the Four Chaplains," *Reader's Digest*, June 1989, pp. 65–70.

28. William Shakespeare, *Much Ado about Nothing*, act 3, scene 2, lines 11–14.

29. Spencer W. Kimball, " 'Why Call Me Lord, Lord, and Do Not the Things Which I Say?' " *Ensign* 5 (May 1975): 7.

30. John Taylor, in *Journal of Discourses* 18:285.

31. John Milton, *Paradise Lost*, book 9, lines 896–99.

32. *Paradise Lost*, book 9, lines 955–59.